Billy Roberts'
10-Step Psychic Development
Programme

Billy Roberts' 10-Step Psychic Development Programme

How to unlock your psychic potential

Billy Roberts

PIATKUS

Copyright © 2003 by Billy Roberts

First published in 2003 by
Judy Piatkus (Publishers) Limited
5 Windmill Street
London W1T 2JA
e-mail: info@piatkus.co.uk

The moral right of the author has been asserted
A catalogue record for this book is available from the British Library

ISBN 0 7499 2449 7

Edited by Lizzie Hutchins and Ian Paten
Text design by Jerry Goldie
Illustrated by Rodney Paull

This book has been printed on paper manufactured with respect for the
environment using wood from managed sustainable resources

Data manipulation by
Action Publishing Technology, Gloucester

Printed and bound in Great Britain by
Antony Rowe Ltd, Chippenham

Contents

I dedicate this book to my wife, Sue, and two pussycats, Suki, the elderly Siamese lady of the family, and Jinjy, the boisterous male. Without their cuddles this book would not have been written.

I would also like to dedicate it to Harry, my Old English sheepdog (now deceased), and also Lucky (also deceased), two of the most important doggie friends I have ever been fortunate to have. I know they are still with me, still giving me that same old warm reassurance I so badly need when I am feeling down.

Introduction

When I am asked what I do for a living, I always say 'stage psychic and author', but that is not all I do. I also work as a medium, receiving messages from the spirit world, and I am invited to corporate functions, universities and theatres all over the world to lecture, hold workshops and demonstrate my psychic abilities to believers and sceptics alike. I have helped thousands of people from all walks of life to discover their psychic powers and use them to live richer and more fulfilled lives. This is more of a vocation than a profession, and regardless of where I am working I truly feel that I am being guided by angels and by a divine omnipotent force.

It has always been my intention to pass on to others the knowledge I have gained so that the mystery surrounding psychic development may be dispelled once and for all. This 10-step programme will do just that. I have no doubt that it will help you to achieve amazing results within a very short time, as I believe that everyone has some degree of psychic potential.

I'd like to begin by sharing some of my own early psychic experiences and show you how these led me to develop my work.

I have been psychic since I was a child, and it is difficult for me to imagine what it would be like *not* to have psychic experiences. My earliest recollections of psychic phenomena go back to when I was three years old. Seeing people who were 'dead' became commonplace for me, and as I spent my early childhood mostly alone I grew up thinking that my experiences were quite normal and that everyone else had them too. I am often asked how these spirit forms appeared to me, and whether they were transparent, nebulous or vague. When I was a child, they were quite solid and substantial. Even today they very often appear to me as flesh-and-blood people, and seem as solid and substantial as any other living person standing in front of me. However, sometimes they manifest themselves before me as images in space, and then become more solid as my connection with them is strengthened.

When I was three I contracted whooping cough, which developed into an incurable respiratory disease called bronchiectasis. Most of my early years were spent either in Alder Hey Children's Hospital, Liverpool, or laid up for months at a time in bed at home. Looking back, I can now see that I was an extremely quiet and often withdrawn child. I had a vivid imagination, and lived most of my life in a world of fantasy. This was the only way I was able to cope with my debilitating illness and the long periods away from school and the company of other children.

My early psychic abilities were not confined to seeing so-called 'dead' people. I experienced a variety of what I now know to be paranormal phenomena, from out-of-body experiences and telepathic communication to seeing nature spirits and angelic beings. The nature spirits I encountered were never story-book creatures with lithe bodies and gossamer-like wings, but rather minute, translucent, childlike creatures, who amused and uplifted me. Today, when I am asked whether I believe in fairies, I always say 'yes' without hesitation.

Some time around the age of three I became acquainted with a spirit guide whom I knew as Tall Pine. Although TP, as I affectionately called him, was a Native American, he was certainly not the archetypal warrior depicted in traditional Westerns. He always appeared to me as a tall, slenderly built and extremely feminine individual, with long dark hair that fell in two plaits, one on either shoulder. Tall Pine never smiled. He was a solid flesh-and-blood person whose peaceful eyes always seemed to conceal a spirit of mischief and excitement. He is still my spirit guide and mentor. Over the years I have learned a great deal from Tall Pine.

The first out-of-body experience I can recall took place when I was around seven. I was terrified, primarily because I did not know what exactly was happening. I was ill, this time suffering from bronchial pneumonia, and my bed had been brought downstairs to the living room. I had a high fever and felt that very black, demon-like creatures were trying to suffocate me. Suddenly an extremely bright light shone inside my head, and the next moment I was floating somewhere high in the far corner of the room, looking down upon myself feverishly tossing and turning. I stayed up there for quite a while until, without any warning, I found myself back inside my body, eyes wide open and feeling very hungry. I now know this was a near-death experience rather than simply an out-of-body experience, and it was a phenomenon I was to experience on numerous occasions after that when I was very ill.

Around the same time I experienced one of the most significant supernatural events of my life. It was a cold early December evening, and I was playing with a friend, Tommy Edgar, in the front room of the terraced house where I lived with my mother, father and older brother, Alby. I was turning the light on and off, trying to frighten my friend. Then, as I tried to turn the light back on again, there was a popping sound, as though the bulb had blown, and the room remained in darkness. Suddenly, there was a bright glow on the wall on top of an old cabinet. The glow grew in intensity and my friend and I watched in amazement as the figure of a lady in a long flowing gown became visible. My friend was terrified and ran from the room crying. The commotion brought my mother and Aunt Sadie in to investigate. I remember my mother's face as she entered the room, and my aunt standing in awe, eyes wide. My mother had inherited psychic abilities from her own mother, but my aunt had always been sceptical of such things. Yet they had both seen the figure.

Because I was a sickly child my mother somehow thought that the apparition had come to make me well. She led me towards the 'Lady of Light' and told me to reach out and touch her. As I did so, the light became more intense, then there was the popping sound again and the room fell into complete darkness for an instant before the overhead light came back on of its own accord. The Lady of Light had gone, leaving a film of pink iridescent powder on the surface of the cabinet. My mother collected the powder in an empty tablet bottle and asked the nuns from a local convent to visit. They duly came and prayed in the room, then asked my mother to show them the powder. I remember watching intently with the nuns as my mother carefully unscrewed the top from the bottle – but it was empty! The contents had disappeared without trace.

For many years we believed that the apparition was that of Our Lady, though it did precede a sequence of very sad and traumatic events in our family. Thankfully, we got through them all, and today the Lady of Light is nothing more than a warm, reassuring memory.

Apparitions didn't manifest themselves to me every day, but I did have other psychic experiences. Up until the age of 12 I was able to tune in to some people's thoughts, almost as you would tune a radio to a specific frequency. This caused me some anguish, as I could tell who really liked me and who did not! My mother and I also had a telepathic relationship, but she was able to read my thoughts better than I could read hers. Perhaps this was simply due to her being a mother! Although this skill subsided somewhat as I reached my teens, telepathy is the fundamental principle underlying the process of mediumship, and so it still forms an integral part of my work.

I also used to delight in watching a multi-coloured vapour surrounding flowers, trees and people. It fascinated me to see that this varied in intensity from person to person. The degree of colour and light showed a person's nature and enabled me to glean detailed information about them. Although, when I was a young child, no one ever explained the aura to me or showed me how to make a detailed analysis of it, I was able to do so intuitively, almost as though I had been born with an innate knowledge of the whole process. We will look at this phenomenon later in the programme.

My psychic abilities began to change once I reached the age of 15. Although puberty can affect the psychic sensitivity, I am quite certain now that this change was primarily because my mind had turned in another direction: I wanted to be the lead guitarist in a Liverpool band. I was preoccupied with my life as a professional musician for approximately eight to ten years, and for at least three years of this period my life was somehow bereft of psychic experiences.

By the time I left school at the age of 16, I was living the life that so many other kids my age only dreamed of. I followed my dream to the Continent, playing alongside some of the biggest names in the world of music. In the mid-sixties I lived for a while in Brussels and played at the 1966 World Fair, supporting such famous names as the Yardbirds, the Moody Blues and the veteran blues singer Memphis Slim. We moved to Paris and played regularly at the famous Locomotive Club next to the Moulin Rouge. It was there that my band supported rock 'n' roll giant Chuck Berry. My fondest memory of working in Paris was meeting my guitar hero, Jimi Hendrix. This has to be one of the most exciting experiences of my life as a musician, and one that I will never forget. I remember thinking that he was quite different from all the others and not going to live very long. In fact Jimi died of a drug overdose in 1970.

They do say that if you can remember the sixties you weren't there. Well, I was there and I do remember most of it. It was an exciting time for me. However, at the height of the so-called 'Flower Power' era, like so many other people involved in the rock music industry, I began to experiment with mind-altering drugs and was introduced to LSD. Today I am sometimes asked whether my experience with drugs caused the further development of my psychic skills. The answer to this has to be 'no'; if anything, my experience with drugs hindered my progress. I have no doubt whatsoever that certain drugs do open the psychic faculties, but without spiritual knowledge to give the necessary foundation such experiences can have an adverse effect. While I did learn from my drug experiences, I gained far more spiritually from my involvement with music.

I toured Europe until 1970, when disaster struck. My father, who had always been a pillar of strength to the family, was diagnosed with pancreatic cancer and died within two months. His death affected me more than anyone ever knew. My drug abuse worsened, and I soon found myself addicted to a wide range of narcotic substances. Needless to say, my career as a musician hit the downward slope, and by 1971 I was living in a bedsit in the suburbs of Liverpool, extremely ill, depressed and alone. I had lost all my confidence and self-respect. My whole world had fallen apart, and I could see no point in carrying on with my life.

The rapid deterioration in my health had aggravated my chronic respiratory disease, and I became so ill that I had to be admitted to hospital for treatment. I then spent months convalescing at my mother's home, and although eventually my body was free of drugs the emotional aftermath felt worse than the addiction itself. I was an emotional and psychological wreck, and found myself desperately in need of guidance. It was then that I experienced divine intervention. There seems no other way to describe it.

It was a clear but blustery November afternoon, and I was sitting quietly in front of the fire, listening to my dog Lucky snoring and allowing my thoughts to wander back over the past couple of years. I felt very relaxed – more so than I had for a long time. However, this overwhelming sense of peace did not last. I began to experience an uncomfortable feeling in my stomach which quickly spread in a straight line up to my chest and then to my head. I began to panic, and sat bolt upright in my chair. I could feel my heart pounding hard against my ribs, and for a moment I thought I was going to die. This feeling of panic soon subsided, and then I could feel my whole body floating, although physically I did not move from the chair. The room was filled with a yellow, pulsating light that made everything seem vibrant and alive. I was transfixed, and again thought that I was going to die. Images of people, places and significant events in my life were flashing across the room. Then suddenly everything stopped and the room fell silent. My whole body seemed to tingle, and for the first time in months I felt well and full of energy. More than this, I felt that I really wanted to live.

This was definitely the critical turning point in my life. Once I accepted that I had a spiritual vocation to fulfil, every area of my life was transformed. My health improved, my outlook became much more positive, and as my own attitude changed, so other people's attitudes towards me also changed. Life started looking up. This was my spiritual metamorphosis.

Later, like most mediums, I developed my natural abilities further by serving an apprenticeship on the Spiritualist church circuit. Although initially I badly wanted to be a healer and not a medium, over the years my psychic experiences made it clear that my path was to lead me in a different direction. I began my career as a comparatively young medium in 1980, serving Spiritualist churches all over the UK and Ireland. My approach was unconventional, and at times radical. I combined Eastern and Western concepts and created a unique method which took the mystery out of psychic development and made it more accessible to everyone. I still use this approach today – it is the very basis of the psychic development course.

By 1983 I began to feel that I was simply preaching to the converted in the Spiritualist church, and began to become disillusioned with the whole Spiritualist scene, feeling that it was rather cliquey. It seemed to me that the majority of those who attended Spiritualist churches were already convinced that there was life beyond death; I desperately wanted to reach those who were either unsure or simply did not believe. I wanted to prove to the sceptics the continuity of the soul beyond death. I also wanted to help other people to become psychic. I established the Thought Workshop, the North-west's very first centre for psychic studies and alternative therapies, in Rodney Street in Liverpool – the Harley Street of the

North! I offered a holistic programme with a broad appeal and the opportunity for people to develop their psychic skills.

The Thought Workshop disbanded some years ago, but today I hold workshops and seminars in psychic study centres, colleges and universities all over the world. I am frequently invited to corporate events, where my methods are used to heighten awareness and improve the performance of the workforce. My psychic stage shows are also very much in demand.

In the summer of 2002, an old friend and I set up Robuck Promotions, incorporating the Billy Roberts Paranormal Study Centre. Robuck Promotions is a unique agency with the largest and most comprehensive register of psychics and mediums in the UK, while the Billy Roberts Paranormal Study Centre offers courses and workshops for all those interested in the paranormal and related subjects. We have some of the most knowledgeable esoteric speakers in the country, and psychics and mediums are in attendance to give consultations every day of the week. In our offices in Liverpool's famous Penny Lane we hold courses and workshops for all those interested in psychic development.

In recounting my own early experiences, I am not suggesting that you need to be extremely ill before psychic development can take place (although it is true that most mediums I know have had problematic lives in one way or another, suffering either emotional problems or physical illness), nor am I advocating the use of mind-altering substances to produce a psychic and spiritual transformation. What I am saying is that when the soul has been drawn to the depths of despair, for whatever reason, it becomes far more aware of an omnipotent, omnipresent power.

This is not to say that a perfectly healthy person cannot develop psychic skills. On the contrary, everyone has the potential to be psychic, and my 10-step programme will help you develop your abilities safely and effectively. Regardless of whether or not you think you are psychic, developing your hidden powers will help you to become more focused and more intuitive, and offer you a much more positive perspective on life.

I have used this programme in many countries, both with students seeking to develop their psychic skills and businessmen wishing to gain greater control of their lives. I have been amazed at the results it has produced and the lives it has transformed. Thousands of people have attended my classes over the past 25 years, and I can honestly say that few have been disappointed.

Many people who read books such as this or attend 'psychic shows' mistakenly think that psychic development is for other people and not for them. I want to show you that you *can* unleash your own psychic powers safely and easily, even from the comfort of your armchair!

You may want to develop your psychic abilities for the first time as a consequence of a spontaneous spiritual awakening in later life, or perhaps simply out of a deep desire to expand your mind. Whatever has brought you to undertake psychic development, my programme will help you to reach your full psychic potential.

Even the so-called 'natural psychic' must cultivate and learn to control their abilities. Lack of discipline is just like having a radio with no tuning dial. All the programmes are there, but without the appropriate controls nothing can be heard.

In my case, my childhood illness encouraged me to be far more focused than a healthy child would be. For another, because my recreational life was so restricted, I became very observant and developed a great depth of concentration – prerequisites of a good psychic. You will learn how to improve your own concentration and observational skills as part of this programme.

My 10-step programme has enabled people from all walks of life to discover their psychic potential and has been responsible for the development of hundreds of mediums and healers. Now it's your turn.

Starting Off

I know only too well that when someone first embarks upon psychic development it can seem strange and sometimes difficult. But my programme will guide you safely through the process. Some of the most unlikely people have used it with great success. One such person is today my business partner and closest friend.

STEVE'S STORY

When I first met him, Steve Buckley was a taxi driver, down-to-earth and with a typical Liverpudlian sense of humour. He had been brought up as a Jehovah's Witness, but had rejected their teachings when he was 15. He came to one of my shows some 14 years ago with the sole intention of proving it to be all nonsense. He was quite certain it was nothing more than trickery and fabrication. Little did he know that my show was to change his whole life.

As soon as I saw this six-foot-four figure walk into the hall with a cocky, almost arrogant self-assurance, I thought, Oh no ... However, Tall Pine said to me, 'This man will help you in the future and will become your friend and great support.' I wasn't convinced – although Tall Pine had never been wrong in his assessments of situations and people, I thought to myself, There's a first time for everything!

In fact, that first night, after I had given my demonstration, Steve's attitude changed dramatically. Over the months that followed he regularly attended my shows and gradually began to get involved in their organisation.

In the years that followed, as well as helping with my shows, Steve attended my training workshops, and gradually began to develop rudimentary signs of mediumship. At this point I must admit it had not occurred to me that there was any chance of him ever becoming a working medium, nor did I think that this was what he wanted. Although he was always extremely attentive at my workshops and lectures, and was always the first to correctly respond to the questions with which I often conclude my day workshops, the truth is I did not see Steve working as a medium before an audience. I was wrong. In 2002 Steve and I went into partnership and set up Robuck Promotions, and today Steve is being prepared for his debut as a medium on the big stage. He has come on in leaps and bounds, and has an inimitable style that makes him stand out from other psychics and mediums. Steve's story is perhaps the best example of how my 10-step psychic development programme works for anyone.

How to Use This Book

During your psychic training programme you will learn more about your psychic nature, how to hone your psychic skills and when to use them, how to protect yourself and your loved ones while engaging in psychic work, how to use your skills for healing or divining the future, and how to develop your own special talents. My holistic approach offers you the chance to maximise your full potential.

In fact my programme is not just appropriate for those wishing to develop their psychic skills, but for everyone who wants to be more positive in their approach to life. I have seen my techniques aid a young man in his recovery from depression and encourage a middle-aged woman who had never really had any confidence to be more assertive. My programme will help you to be more insightful and decisive so you are more efficient at work, and it will help you to be more relaxed at home, bringing balance to your life.

Before you embark on the programme I would advise you to read the book fully. In this way you will be able to familiarise yourself with the techniques so that you can plan how you are going to use the system. Part 1 contains two chapters which outline what psychic powers are and show you how you can plan your training programme to ensure that your own powers develop quickly and safely. They will also give you a good idea of what to expect. In Part 2 we embark on the 10-step programme itself, organised as follows:

Step 1

In the first step you are introduced to your psychic energy systems and learn how to revitalise them in preparation for psychic development.

Step 2

The second step looks at preparing yourself mentally, physically and emotionally.

Step 3

The third step involves improving your concentration and observational skills, which will be invaluable to you in your psychic work.

Step 4

Step four gives you the chance to learn to meditate. Meditation is the most effective means of accessing higher states of consciousness and generating the energy you will need for psychic work.

Step 5

Intuition is also fundamental to psychic experience. Developing and using your intuitive powers in a positive way is step five in your programme.

Step 6

After a review of what we've learned so far, the sixth step examines the specific psychic abilities you might develop, including clairsentience, clairvoyance, clairaudience, remote viewing and psychometry.

Step 7

Moving on from this, we look at receiving information from the spirit world via mediumship and channelling, and also how to strengthen your connection with the energies of the so-called 'dead'.

Step 8

The eighth step examines the different tools you can use for divination, including tea leaves, the crystal ball, the black mirror, candle scrying, palmistry, the Tarot, runes, astrology, dowsing and my very own method of psychic handwriting analysis.

Step 9

Many people hope to use their psychic abilities for healing, and guidelines for both healing and self-healing are offered in the ninth step.

Step 10

The final step outlines how you can protect yourself and those you love throughout your psychic development programme.

The course does not need to be followed in any particular order, though it is important to lay the groundwork and prepare yourself properly, so do read Part 1 thoroughly first. After this, I suggest you choose the methods from Part 2 that appeal to you most, or even integrate parts of the programme into the system you already use. You are not bound by any rules. The programme has been designed to suit all types of people; you may find that some of the exercises do not work for you while others produce positive results. You may rest assured, though, that they are all safe and effective. All you need is patience, determination and a little discipline. Even someone who claims to have no psychic abilities at all will benefit in many ways.

Warning. If you have any history of psychological illness it is best to avoid any serious involvement in the paranormal or psychic development. Psychic development can have a profound effect upon the mind, and may be detrimental to psychological and emotional health if you are not sufficiently robust mentally.

Psychic development will give you more insight into your own personality and enable you to better understand the world around you. It will help you to eliminate negative patterns of thinking and to adopt a more positive approach to any difficulties you encounter. By using my programme you will become more sensitive to the environment around you, and as a consequence will have a closer relationship with the super-sensual world and the invisible forces that guide you.

A recovering alcoholic once successfully used my programme and wrote me a long letter listing his achievements. He said, 'While others raised their glasses in respect of my achievements, I raised my consciousness towards the things I was yet to achieve.'

Let's start by taking a look at what psychic powers really are.

Part 1

Preparation

Chapter 1

What Are Psychic Powers?

Most of us live from day to day unaware of the powers that lie within us, powers that could transform our lives. Yet things are beginning to change. We are seeing an increasing shift in the collective consciousness – humanity as a whole is beginning to reawaken faculties that have lain dormant for thousands of years.

The increase in the number of people attending my workshops and seminars has proved to me how interest in the paranormal has grown. These students have a far greater knowledge of the subject than those of 20 years ago. Whether this is due to the fact that there are more books available today or whether there is a more spiritually significant reason, it is quite apparent that the old attitudes of scepticism and mistrust are being replaced by open-minded curiosity. The spiritual consciousness of the planet is increasing, and people from all walks of life are seeking to develop their psychic powers.

Before you start on your own psychic development programme, I want to give you an idea of exactly what these so-called 'psychic' abilities are, and how you can benefit from developing them.

Definitions

The dictionary definition of 'psychic' covers a broad spectrum: '1) Sensitive to phenomena lying outside the range of normal experience; 2) Of soul or mind; 3) Appearing to be outside the region of physical law.'

Psychic powers include:

worldbooks

Guild House, Farnsby Street, Swindon X, SN99 9XX
Customer Careline Tel: (0870) 1650230

DELIVERY NOTE

MEMBER No: 0092023320

NAME: MISS J WILSON

REF: 9130101536

DATE: 26/11/03

YOUR ORDER DETAILS

2448918	B Roberts 10 Step Psyc	Enclosed
2448611	How Clean is your H.?	Enclosed
2448967	Titanias Crystal Ball	Enclosed

PART DELIVERY

PLEASE RETAIN

CUSTOMER SERVICES

If you have any queries, you can call us on the Customer Careline
(see overleaf).

HOURS OF SERVICE: Monday to Friday 8.30am to 8.30pm
(9.30 to 21.30 Central European Time)

Alternatively write to:-
Customer Service, at the address overleaf
**PLEASE QUOTE YOUR MEMBERSHIP NUMBER
TO ENSURE PROMPT SERVICE**

Please check the contents of the parcel against the details on this Delivery Note. If there is anything missing or incorrect, always contact our Customer Services department who will be pleased to resolve the matter for you. Please enclose the packing slip with any return made. We would also advise you to get a receipt from the Post Office or Carrier.

When do I pay for my books/items?

Please make your cheque or postal order payable to your club quoting your membership number on the reverse. You can also pay by credit card by completing the reverse of the order form.

"Why not ring 0870 1650165, our account information and Orderline, if
you wish to order, make a payment or for simple account enquiries".

PICKING SLIP
CA   009202332O

K26

18321120

Titanias Crystal Ball 2448967 28966   **A050P**
B Roberts 10 Step Psy 2448918 30206   **J395X**
How Clean is your H.? 2448611 32994   **J403B**

2   LINE6   21   2   MP

If you have to return all or part of your order please enclose this slip

00017660

- ◆ Telepathy – mind-to-mind communication
- ◆ Precognition – gaining insights into the future
- ◆ Clairvoyance and clairaudience – seeing and hearing things beyond the natural range of the senses

All these as well as other powers will be covered in more depth in later chapters.

My own skills are a combination of clairvoyance, clairaudience and clairsentience – literally, 'clear seeing', 'clear hearing' and 'clear sensing' – and I am able to use these either simultaneously or independently of each other. However, my predominant ability is clairaudience, the ability to 'hear' sounds beyond the normal range. I either hear a voice inside my head, usually to my left side (because I am slightly deaf in that ear), or receive an extraneous thought. I find the latter a little disconcerting, as it is as though someone else is using my mind to think. Strange, you may think, but that's exactly how it feels.

As regards the voices I hear, at worst they can be quite muffled and almost incoherent, like listening to a radio that is not properly tuned in; at best they come with such clarity that the speaker might well be standing behind me. When I was a child, disembodied voices very often kept me amused for long periods. A lady's voice used to recite nursery rhymes to me and would sometimes even tell me a story. This would continue until I fell asleep.

Although such powers may seem unusual today, they were commonplace to our prehistoric forebears, who relied upon these skills for survival. They were far more psychically attuned to their environment than we are because they functioned at a totally instinctive level. 'Intuition' is often used as an umbrella term to cover a wide range of psychic skills. Although strictly speaking it is not a psychic skill itself, developing it will strengthen your psychic abilities. In Step 5 we will explore how intuition can be used to enhance awareness and to develop the other psychic senses.

It is important that you start the psychic development programme without any preconceived ideas about which skills you will develop. My holistic approach will ensure that you will cultivate the skills that are right for you.

Research into Psychic Experiences

I am quite sure that there is less of a stigma attached to the paranormal now than when I was a child in the fifties. Nonetheless, a minority still views the subject with disdain and cynicism, particularly in the United Kingdom. Most research has taken place in America and Russia, where it is all regarded more seriously. However, very little is still known about how psychic experiences are actually produced.

Some years ago now I was subjected to numerous scientific tests. While I was functioning psychically, my brain waves were monitored by an electroencephalograph (EEG) and my arms and fingers connected to a biofeedback apparatus to measure skin resistance. The results were quite astounding. Although at the beginning of the experiment the oscillation of the biofeedback machine showed that I was far from relaxed, once I began to demonstrate my abilities this changed dramatically. The high-pitched tone subsided to a monotonous drone, while the graph produced by the EEG changed from a consistent pattern to one that was extremely erratic. My pupils were very dilated and my heart rate dropped considerably. There was no doubt that significant physiological and psychological changes had occurred while I was focused psychically.

Scientists don't know exactly what's going on, but for thousands of years Eastern sages have maintained that all spiritual experiences take place within the pineal gland, the small walnut-shaped gland deep in the centre of the brain. Recent research has established that the pineal gland is larger in a child than in an adult, and more developed in the female than the male. This probably accounts for the fact that traditionally children are very psychic, and women much more psychically attuned than men. Research has also shown that the development of psychic abilities somehow increases the size of the pineal gland. It is thought that some form of abnormal organ-isation is taking place in the brain and nerve centres of a fully developed psychic, and that there is some activation of the so-called 'old brain' situated at the back of the skull. What is definitely known is that psychic abilities may be developed by specifically designed exercises or triggered by emotional, psychological or physical trauma. During my 10-step programme you will have the chance to try out such exercises for yourself.

Incidentally, Christopher Reardon, a Canadian scientist, has concluded that all paranormal experiences are purely subjective and that the human brain is the architect of all such phenomena. In fact he wondered whether phenomena of any kind took place outside the human psyche. In some ways this is a Buddhist concept – that the external world is Maya, Illusion, and that reality manifests itself only in the mind.

Latent Psychic Powers

Most people, whether they consider themselves psychic or not, have had some form of paranormal experience at some time in their lives – suddenly sensing danger for no apparent reason, for example, or sensing an unseen presence.

PETER'S STORY

An example of someone with latent psychic powers is Peter, a 19-year-old man suffering from cystic fibrosis. Although the prognosis is not very promising with this condition, quality of life can be improved in more ways than one. I had special sympathy for Peter because the condition from which I have suffered since I was three is actually a symptom of cystic fibrosis. Peter's condition was fairly stable, but he had suddenly become extremely depressed and was overwhelmed by a morbid fear of dying.

Peter was extremely intelligent, with a flair for painting. His creative talent was quite remarkable, and he had a special aptitude for sketching faces, a skill that I was certain could be used in a psychic way. I asked him whether he knew what a psychic artist was. To my amazement, he did. It was then that I discovered that he often saw the faces of 'dead' relatives just as he was falling asleep. I found this interesting, as when someone has an inherent clairvoyant skill this is one of the ways in which it manifests itself.

Peter was able to attend workshops at my centre in Rodney Street, and over the course of several weeks I worked closely with him, using the methods described in this book. In a very short period this talented young man came on in leaps and bounds. His excellent portraiture skill developed even more, and it became apparent to me that, as well as being a talented artist, he was a natural medium. More than this, though, his attitude towards death and his debilitating illness changed completely. Until he passed away two years later, he frequently demonstrated his unusual ability, accurately sketching faces of the so-called 'dead'. Once this skill developed fully it transformed his way of thinking and made him far more focused. He knew that he was going to die, but his psychic skill convinced him that death was not the end.

Supernatural abilities can arise unbidden even late in life. Joan Briggs is a prime example. She consulted me on a matter of 'extreme importance', as she put it to me on the telephone. Although I was extremely busy at the time, the urgency in her voice left me no alternative but to invite her to my home.

JOAN'S STORY

Joan was an articulate, well-spoken lady in her late sixties. She seemed extremely nervous and more than a little embarrassed as she began telling me her story. Although dressed in everyday attire, she told me that she had been a nun since she was 20. One day she was making her way from the small chapel in the convent towards an adjacent room when she slipped on a newly polished floor and fell over backwards. Her head made contact with the floor, and that was the last thing she remembered. Although her fall resulted in a short stay in hospital, her injuries were minimal and she recovered fully within two weeks. At that point I assumed that she had come to me for healing, but there was more ...

Within days of being discharged from hospital Joan began to hear disembodied voices, which sounded to her like two people having a conversation in the room next door. However, when she listened carefully she recognised the voices as those of her deceased mother and father, whom she had loved dearly. As the days passed the voices became clearer, and Joan found that she could not only hear exactly what they were saying to her, but also hold a conversation with them. She quite openly admitted to me that her experiences had caused her to doubt her own sanity, and that she really thought her fall had caused some damage to her brain which had somehow gone undetected. But then she began to 'see' her 'dead' parents, leaving no doubt in her mind that she was not mad but was having supernatural experiences.

I was able to offer Joan the reassurance and guidance that she so badly needed, and before she left I asked her who had referred her to me. She smiled and said, 'Sister Virginia.' I felt a shiver pass through my body, as Sister Virginia was a young nun who had helped me when I was in my late twenties. During a period of great distress, I had turned to her on the advice of an elderly friend. The kindly nun had said quite categorically that my gifts were God-given, and that one day I must use them for the very reason that they had been given to me – to help others.

Over the years Joan and I became good friends. Although she remained in the convent, right up until her death at the age of 82 she too was able to use her psychic skills to help others.

Joan's psychic abilities were precipitated by physical trauma – they had probably always been there, and it took physical shock to jolt them into action, so to speak – but the point I want to make is that psychic skills can manifest themselves for any number of reasons. Even if you appear to have no psychic abilities whatsoever, I can assure you that you do have latent psychic talents, and they can be cultivated and refined by following my 10-step programme.

Inherited Powers

There is quite a lot of evidence to suggest that psychic abilities are handed down through a family, often skipping a generation and sometimes being transferred from one gender to the other.

In my own case the ability appears to have originated on my mother's side of the family and with the female line. According to my mother, my grandmother had a number of psychic experiences. At the very end of the Second World War she was sitting quietly in front of the fire when she heard the voice of her son, who was serving in Burma, saying, 'Oh, Mam ...' Immediately she knew that he had been killed. Some months after the war had ended, my grandmother had a visit from a soldier who had been with my uncle when he died. He confirmed that as the sniper's bullet rang out across the jungle her beloved son had called out, 'Oh, Mam ...', just as my grandmother had heard while relaxing in her chair on the other side of the world.

When two people are so 'in tune' in this way, they may not only be aware of each other's distress, but may also be able to read each other's thoughts. Should one die, the other often believes the telepathic relationship has gone for ever. It hasn't! At death it becomes more distinct and very often much more profound. So if you are going about your daily chores and suddenly a 'dead' friend or relative comes to mind for no apparent reason, it may be because they are actually there and attempting to make their presence felt. Most people dismiss this experience as being no more than a sentimental memory, but in the majority of cases it is a discarnate loved one endeavouring to make telepathic contact.

Inherited powers may not last, however. When my son Ben was three years old I was driving with him through the Sefton Park area of Liverpool, near the former home of a good friend called Nelly. Nelly was an elderly medium who had been on dialysis for the last few years of her life and had sadly passed away when Ben was only six months old. She was one of those wise people we occasionally meet at the right time in our lives, and was someone for whom I had had the greatest respect.

As we passed Nelly's old house, I thought how nice it would if we could call on her, as I used to, for a chat and a cup of tea. At that moment Ben broke his long, thoughtful silence: 'Who's Nelly, Daddy?' I felt a sudden chill pass through my body, and I pulled over and stopped the car. 'Why did you ask that?' I asked. 'My head is speaking to me,' he replied. He placed his hands on either side of his head and for a moment looked confused. 'My head speaks to me.'

Not wanting to distress my son in any way, I immediately began talking about other things. However, later on I discovered that this was something he had experienced often. In fact, this was exactly the way in which my own abilities manifested themselves to me as a child. In my case the phenomenon remained with me. With Ben it stopped when he reached nine years of age.

Precognition

One of the gifts that appears to have come down through my family to me is that of precognition. For example, in 1969 I contracted pneumonia and was confined to bed for two weeks. I faced away from the window, which was behind me. One beautiful autumnal morning the sun was cascading through the window, filling my room with bright light. The lace curtains cast a shadow on the wall. As I watched the patterns moving with the sun, the shadow suddenly became a newspaper. I sat forward in bed to take a closer look. I could see the name of the newspaper, which was unknown to me. I was amazed to be able to read a headline: 'Albert Edward Roberts died on 16 May 1970 at the age of 66'.

I felt cold and climbed out of bed to take a closer look, but as I did so the sun moved behind the clouds and the image of the newspaper faded. Then, as the sun came out again, the newspaper reappeared, this time turned to the second page. This was even stranger. The text was Chinese, in vertical columns. There was a photograph of an elderly monastic figure. Then the sun moved behind the clouds once again and this time the newspaper faded completely.

I climbed back into bed and just sat there, turning the experience over and over in my mind. My thoughts were suddenly interrupted as my father, Albert, came into the room with a cup of tea for me. He probably wondered why I was staring at him so intently. He was an extremely strong man and had been blessed with good health, never having been ill in his life. As for the oriental monk, I had no idea who he was. I dismissed the whole experience and attributed it to the antibiotics I had been taking.

When my father was diagnosed with pancreatic cancer in April 1970, I tried desperately not to think about my experience with the newspaper. However, the more I tried, the more vividly it came into my thoughts. My father duly died on 16 May 1970 at the age of 66.

I did not find out who the oriental monk was until 1977. He appeared to me shortly after a period of meditation, introducing himself as Zalom, one of three spiritual helpers of mine. I have had no contact with him since that day.

The question is, why was I shown the newspaper? Why did I need to know about my father's death? Similar questions are often asked by people who come to my workshops. It seems that precognitive experiences are quite common, particularly in dreams. 'Dead' relatives may also appear to warn about approaching disasters. It has become clear to me that precognitive experiences never reveal happy events – perhaps they are intended as a form of preparation.

Out-of-body Experiences

People who come to my workshops have experienced a wide range of other 'unusual' phenomena, from seeing faces in the patterns of curtains and carpets to out-of-body experiences, many of which have taken place during surgery.

A most unusual out-of-body story was related to me by a young Liverpool policeman. He had cornered a burglar, who threw a brick into his face and knocked him out. Instantly he was projected from his body and was able to see himself lying unconscious on the cold wet ground. Thinking that he was dead, he watched calmly as his body was carried into an ambulance and taken to hospital. He told me that while he was hovering somewhere outside his body he found himself gravitating to where the perpetrator of the crime lived. After some surgery and a spell in hospital he recovered fully and was able to give the exact location of the man who had committed the crime. No doubt his story was more credible because he was a policeman, and a very level-headed and down-to-earth one at that.

Know your 'Psychic Quotient' – PQ

To start you on the road to developing your psychic potential, here is a test to see where you are now. Answer the following questions as honestly as you can.

Section One   Yes   No

1. Do you feel an affinity with some people more than others? ☐ ☐

2. Do you sometimes have strong feelings about imminent events, perhaps an inner voice telling you something is wrong? ☐ ☐

	Yes	No
3. Do you sometimes find yourself daydreaming in the middle of a conversation with someone, even though you are not bored?	☐	☐
4. Do you sometimes have vivid dreams about impending doom and disaster?	☐	☐
5. Do sweet or unusual fragrances sometimes remind you of someone who is dead?	☐	☐
6. Do you ever see images when staring at a carpet or curtains?	☐	☐
7. Do you sometimes think you can hear someone calling your name when you know you are alone in the house?	☐	☐
8. When lying in bed, do you ever feel pressure on top of the covers, as though someone were sitting on the end of the bed?	☐	☐
9. Have you experienced déjà vu on more than one occasion?	☐	☐
10. When drifting off to sleep, do you see small faces passing quickly in front of you?	☐	☐

Score

How many times did you say 'yes'?

1–3   Patience and determination will be needed. However, this programme will help you to realise your potential.

4–6   Your psychic abilities need a little encouragement.

7–10 You have already developed psychic abilities.

Section Two Yes No

1. When engrossed in conversation, are you able to listen ☐ ☐
   to dialogue taking place between other people?

2. When talking to someone, do you sometimes find your ☐ ☐
   attention wandering away from the conversation, yet
   still know exactly what has been said?

3. When drifting off to sleep, do you ever feel as though ☐ ☐
   you are floating?

4. Have you ever woken up in the middle of the night ☐ ☐
   and been aware of just having had a conversation with
   someone?

5. Do you sometimes experience the sensation of wearing ☐ ☐
   a hat or spectacles, though you wear neither?

6. Have you ever stopped someone in the street, ☐ ☐
   overwhelmed by a feeling of familiarity, only to find
   that you've never met them before?

7. Have you ever felt you've lived before? ☐ ☐

8. Have you ever held an object in your hands and ☐ ☐
   experienced strong feelings of joy or sadness?

9. Do you know when a thunderstorm is approaching, ☐ ☐
   even when the day is quite clear?

10. Do people always want to tell you their problems and ☐ ☐
    look upon you as a sort of 'confessor'?

Score

   1–3 A greater-than-average psychic potential.

   4–6 Immense psychic potential.

   7–10 Exceptional!

How did you do? Whether you feel you have a long way to go or have already developed psychic abilities, you will benefit from my 10-step programme. But before we see how we can make it work for you, let's consider how you should plan your training programme.

Chapter 2

Planning Your Programme

When starting out on your psychic training programme you will be entering new and unknown territory. You should first decide exactly what you are seeking to achieve through your psychic development, so that you at least have some idea in which direction you are heading.

Answer the following questions as honestly as you can.

Psychic Training Questionnaire

1. Are you hoping to use your psychic abilities professionally?

2. Is it your intention to use your psychic abilities only for your own amusement?

3. Are your psychic abilities already developed and do you wish to refine them?

4. Are you seeking to develop your psychic abilities to make money?

5. Do you hope to use your psychic abilities to help others?

6. Do psychic abilities run in your family? If you don't feel that you're psychic yourself, do you nonetheless want to follow the genetic trend?

7. Are you seeking to develop your psychic abilities simply because you are interested in the process and are not very bothered whether or not your abilities develop? (Some people are only interested in the methodology with no desire to use their psychic skills publicly.)

8. Are you seeking to develop psychic skills or the skills of a medium, and do you know the difference?

My answers

1. If it is your intention to use your psychic abilities professionally, you should be aware that you will require much more than psychic skills to make a living. It takes time to build up a respectable clientele and to be able to arrange sufficient consultations to enable you to give up your nine-to-five job. You will need to be extremely patient. Apart from advertising in the appropriate journals, recommendation is the most effective way of expanding your clientele, and this takes time. The more confidence you have in your psychic skills, the more your clients will trust you. This in itself is a confidence-building exercise that will improve your psychic abilities.

2. Although there is absolutely nothing wrong with developing your psychic abilities for your own amusement, you will probably find that once you have developed the skills you will want others to share them with you. Besides, when you consider all the effort needed to develop psychic abilities, keeping them to yourself is pretty pointless.

3. Most people assume that because a psychic skill is already apparent no further effort is required, but psychic development is always an ongoing process.

4. Should money be your sole motivation, then this will most definitely be reflected in your work. Besides, psychic work should be more of a vocation, and although you need money to survive, you will never attain great spiritual heights if you are solely money oriented.

5. I have known numerous psychics and mediums whose only desire was to use their abilities to help others. This is highly

commendable. However, you *do* have to exercise common sense, as there are those who will take you for granted and abuse your kindness and compassion. By all means use your psychic skills to help others, but always be alert for those who do not really need your help and seek only to exploit your abilities.

6. The fact that someone in your family is psychic does not mean that you automatically have a natural psychic talent. Although psychic abilities tend to run in families, they do sometimes skip a generation or two and are not apparent in every family member. Although I possess a psychic skill, my elder brother does not.

7. It is sometimes quite unhealthy to involve yourself in a strict psychic development regime when your motives are unfocused. There has to be more than an interest in the paranormal when seeking to develop psychically. Apart from this, unless you inwardly feel that there *is* something to develop, too much effort would be required and very little achieved.

8. Psychic abilities are far easier to cultivate than those associated with mediumship, and although mediums are psychic, psychics are not mediums. A medium is someone who has the ability to receive information from the so-called 'dead', while a psychic is someone who has the ability to obtain information about both future and past events.

The Importance of Spiritual Understanding

Psychic development initiates profound mental and emotional changes, and in order to cope with these changes you need to have some sort of spiritual grounding. This does not mean attending church, or for that matter becoming holy and pious. But when you are endeavouring to cultivate psychic skills, you need a code of ethics with which to work. Without this deeper spiritual understanding you can never reach your full psychic potential.

To me, 'spiritual understanding' means a broadening of consciousness to encompass being aware of life itself and of every living thing. Increased awareness also brings responsibility. The more your psychic skills develop, the more you should be aware of your responsibilities towards those who consult you. There are some people who will have immense respect for everything you tell them and will live their life according to the guidance you give them. You must realise this from the very beginning and give a great deal of thought to the advice you offer.

It is also important to learn as much as possible. Knowledge leads to experience and wisdom.

Background Research

Before I became a professional psychic I visited as many psychics as I could, all over the British Isles. I wanted to witness their different styles and techniques so that I had some idea of how exactly to present my own skill when the time was right. This extensive investigation lasted over two years, during which time I made some good friends as well as a lot of useful contacts. Before taking the first steps in your own programme it would also be a beneficial exercise for you to see as many psychics and mediums as possible. At least this way you will have a reasonable idea of how different people use their skills.

Although reading books on the subject is extremely important, it should be borne in mind that books offer only guidelines on which avenue to pursue and which techniques are the most effective. These methods may not work for you. It is therefore important to assemble as many ideas as possible so that you can create your own programme. Even books that contain what may seem like far-out concepts should not be dismissed lightly, as however extreme they seem they are likely to be based on traditional ideas and will definitely work for some people.

You will find that my 10-step programme has been designed to suit most needs and is a mixture of Eastern and Western concepts with a very broad appeal.

Working with Others or 'Sitting Alone'

During your training you have the choice of working alone or seeking an appropriate group to help you with your development.

Although many people warn against so-called 'sitting alone' in the early stages of psychic development, I always tell my students that as long as they abide by all the rules and exercise great caution, then sitting alone should present no problems at all. Should you be of a nervous disposition, however, then it is best to find a good teacher or a suitable group of people with whom you feel comfortable. In the initial stages of development, particularly unsupervised, there is always the danger of a rogue spirit attaching itself to you, or even the possibility of your being forced into a trance-like state, so it is important that when sitting alone you maintain self-control at all times. (For more on psychic protection, see Step 10.)

If you feel you would be more comfortable in a group, the first step is to check out psychic journals, newspapers and magazines. I am a columnist for *Psychic World* newspaper, which is an ideal place in which to look for an appropriate group. I believe in the ancient precept 'when the student is ready, the teacher will always appear'.

Try not to be too hasty in joining a group. Find out as much as you can about it first. Working in a group is very interesting and often more exciting than working alone, but it must consist of people with whom you feel perfectly in tune. Groups can introduce an element of pressure and competition and often breed envy and jealousy, which are very unproductive and defeat the whole object of psychic development. It is quite acceptable to try a group out for a month or so before committing yourself completely. The other members should understand why you are doing this.

Whether you have decided to work alone or in a group, your programme needs to be carefully designed and must contain a mixture of practical exercises and meditation. Although a lot of your ideas may come from other people, it is always best to create your own exercises and to experiment as much as possible. Use my programme as a basis, and then try integrating other concepts to create your own regime.

If you have chosen to work alone, there is no harm in allowing a friend to help you occasionally. And at the end of each month your progress should be assessed, if possible by someone knowledgeable in the subject.

Remember that, should you have any history of psychological illness, it is always best to avoid any serious involvement in the paranormal or psychic development, as it may be detrimental to your health.

Structuring Your Programme

As already mentioned, once you have prepared yourself fully for psychic development you can either work through the book in sequential order or just randomly select exercises to suit your requirements at the time.

To recap, the first two steps involve preparation:

1. Learning about your psychic nature.
2. Preparing yourself mentally, physically and emotionally.

I would recommend that you always start with these, as they lay the foundations for your future development. Then, once you are ready, you can go on to develop your psychic skills in more depth by following the next steps.

Proceed at your own pace. It is always better to go slowly but surely rather than overdo it, particularly in the initial stages of the programme.

It is important to structure your training programme comfortably around your day. Allow yourself one hour to begin with and then increase this once you are more confident about performing the exercises.

Remember, the programme is not a punishment, so do not make it a labour by forcing yourself to go through the exercises. Mental exhaustion is self-destructive and will not produce any benefits at all. Pace yourself and try not to be too impatient.

Keep a record of the results of each exercise. When I began my own development I would always make a note of the exercises I had used and what experiences they had produced. I would analyse the exercises that did not seem to work for me and would make appropriate changes to them, modifying them until positive results were obtained. For example, I always found that psychometrising small items of jewellery did not really work for me, but the process *did* work when I applied it to larger objects, such as a handbag or even a piano. You may find that your skills will only work when applied in a certain way. Try a process of elimination until you discover your true forte. And it's best not to have any preconceived ideas about what that might be.

JOHN'S STORY

Ten years ago I was taking a series of workshops in Manchester and was constantly interrupted by one of the few men attending that day. He was a little too confident and kept contradicting me. His problem was that he wanted desperately to be a medium and he was adamant that this was the route he would take. I made several attempts to explain that my holistic approach meant that he might possibly develop other skills, but he had his own ideas on the subject. At the conclusion of the workshop I was sure that he was not a medium in the normal sense of the word, but rather was a natural healer. When I told him what I thought, he took umbrage. We parted company with him getting quite irate and telling me in no uncertain terms what he thought of me and my assessment of his psychic skills. He wanted to be a medium and that was that!

Some years later I was taking a one-day seminar in London when I was approached by a middle-aged lady. 'I would like you to meet someone,' she said, smiling. 'John Brady is one of our top healers.' A tall man took my hand in a vice-like grip and shook it until I lost all feeling in it. It wasn't until he actually spoke that I realised who he was – the cocky man who had wanted to be a medium and nothing else. He now had a thick, greying beard, but there was no mistaking the resonant tones of his rich voice. He smiled sheepishly and said, 'You were right after all, Billy. I'm a healer, and I love every minute of it.' And although I didn't say it out loud, I thought, I told you so!

Initial Energy Changes

During the initial stages of development of the psychic faculties there is often a predominance of female energy, and male students may become more sensitive and emotional at this time. While female students are usually unaffected emotionally by this predominance of female energy, they can often experience psychological changes which may cause some unpredictable mood swings and bouts of depression. However, once the faculties are fully developed, the psychological and emotional make-up of both men and women usually returns to normal.

I must reiterate again at this point that psychic development encourages only what is already within a person, and *does not* cause unnatural changes to occur. However, because of the changes that take place in the brain and nerve centres, it is important that there should be no history of psychological problems, as psychic development may make the condition worse.

Working Safely

Before you begin your psychic work you would be well advised to ask for protection and guidance.

Whether you are religious or not, the power of prayer must not in any way be underestimated. Owing to my mother's influence I have prayed devotedly since I was a small child, and know that there can be great power in it. The Lord's Prayer in particular has deep mystic significance, and was helping people long before Jesus used it. It is a universal mantra with great power and meaning. Used often enough it will be absorbed by the subconscious mind and will afford you the protection you need during your development.

Should prayer not appeal to you, you could create your own personal mantra. This can be anything from the words 'Protect me, keep me safe!' to the accepted word 'Light'. By chanting these words over and over you will bring strength and power to your subconscious mind. However, in order for a mantra to afford you the protection you need, it must be repeated regularly and integrated into your daily meditation procedure (see Step 4).

It goes without saying that you should always avoid alcohol and drugs before applying yourself to the programme. These not only impair the senses, but also create negative energy in your aura. This can be detrimental to your mental well-being during your training.

For other methods of psychic protection, see Step 10.

Exercise Common Sense

It is always wise in psychic development to exercise common sense and know your limitations. I remember in the very early stages of my own development being so fascinated with the things I was experiencing that they occupied most of my time. I eventually became extremely nervous and had difficulty in sleeping. As time passed by I became anxious and quite depressed.

This situation improved only when I joined a development circle and was taken under the wing of Sylvia Alexio, a veteran medium and well-respected teacher. A development circle is the Spiritualist training process for mediums. The students, or 'sitters', are usually supervised by a medium or suitably trained person. At my development circle, Sylvia told me in no uncertain terms that I had to be more disciplined and learn to structure my development programme. I followed her advice and within three months my condition greatly improved.

Seek Support

In the early stages of psychic development it is not uncommon for the student to experience periods of depression and a desire to be alone. These emotions quickly pass, but it always helps to have someone in whom you can confide and who has knowledge of the changes that occur during psychic development.

In my own case I was fortunate to have a very knowledgeable friend who had devoted many years of his life to the development of his psychic faculties. As well as giving me support when I needed it, Desmond Tierney gave me books to read which ultimately proved extremely significant to my development. These are listed in the Further Reading section.

Don't Overuse Your Abilities

All too many psychics abuse their abilities simply by overusing them without any regard for their own health. Using your psychic skills as a party piece to amuse or impress friends is not recommended. Particularly in the initial stages of your development, you should demonstrate your psychic skills only when asked to by someone in a position of authority, and even then it should only be in an appropriate environment as part of a training exercise.

Never demonstrate your developing skills while under the influence of intoxicating substances, such as alcohol or anything else that impairs the senses.

Continuous use of any psychic ability is detrimental to health and may ultimately have psychological repercussions. In the long term it can cause physical health to deteriorate rapidly, and may even place a great deal of stress on the heart. I have witnessed this with young psychics on numerous occasions and, unfortunately, it has been far too late for me to be able to help.

I know from experience that psychics are often invited to parties and other social gatherings primarily to show off their abilities and not because they are a valued friend. Only experience teaches you who is a friend and who is not! Never succumb to flattery, regardless of who is doing the flattering. This applies as much to the experienced psychic as to the less experienced student.

Now you're ready to take the first step in the process of psychic development. The very first thing you need is an understanding of how it all works and how the mind and body are affected. So before we do anything else let's take a look at your psychic nature.

Part 2

The 10-Step Psychic Development Programme

Discover Your Psychic Nature

This first part of the programme is an extremely important part of my training. Knowledge of the subtle anatomy – or psychic nature – is vital to the whole process of psychic development. Although generally speaking it is not part of the traditional approach to development, and people sometimes find some of the concepts difficult to grasp at first, I always include it in my programme, as I know that an understanding of it will be invaluable later on.

First you need to know a little about your own psychic nature and how you interact with the world about you. Our everyday world is interpenetrated by other, more subtle worlds in a multi-dimensional universe, and we ourselves are extremely complex beings, each possessing the psychic potential to transcend physical and mental limitations and to access these far more refined worlds.

The Soul and the Physical Body

In addition to our physical body we also have a soul. For the soul there is no beginning and no end, and the death of the physical body is merely a transition in the soul's endless journey, a period of rest between one phase of life and another.

How exactly the soul arrives in the physical universe to be born in a physical body has baffled the greatest minds throughout time. But it is known that during its descent through the different worlds of the cosmos, it draws to itself sheaths or bodies of matter that allow it to exist at the various levels through which it passes. Eventually it settles in the dense three-dimensional world to sojourn in a physical body. The various energy bodies in which it is clothed enable it to function in an alien environment. These bodies make up the subtle anatomy.

The Subtle Anatomy

The subtle anatomy's responsibility is to maintain our balance while we sojourn in the physical world. It does this through various energy systems.

Although the energy systems of the subtle anatomy and the physical anatomy are quite distinct from each another, one cannot function effectively without the other. The health and well-being of the physical body are dependent upon the unrestricted movement of subtle energy. When the subtle and physical systems are perfectly synchronised, balance is maintained in the physical, mental and spiritual areas of our life.

Prana: The Vital Force

The subtle agent through which life is sustained is known as *prana*. Although in the East this concept has been known for thousands of years, the West has only recently begun to be aware of it. The existence of prana can now be scientifically proved, and the way it affects our bodies clinically substantiated.

Although prana enters the body with each breath, it is not the air we breathe. It is not matter, although it can be seen working through all forms of matter. It interpenetrates the physical body and is responsible for the integration of all living cells into a whole. It is the binding force of the universe.

The more prana we are able to breathe in and retain in our bodies, the better our quality of life. When we are deficient in prana, ultimately we fall into poor health.

Some individuals naturally draw great stores of prana into their bodies. People who work with the earth, such as farmers and gardeners, usually retain large amounts of prana. Those who possess such vitality make powerful healers and are able to pass their energy on to others easily. Simply being in their presence for a few moments is invigorating and can have an uplifting effect when you are feeling under the weather.

When I was in my twenties, I knew an elderly German gentleman who lived in one of four Victorian houses in an adjacent street. He was the local character and always had an interesting story to tell. It was much more than that, though – old Fritz had something about him that I can only describe as 'supernatural'. It didn't matter how miserable or ill I felt when I met him, just being in the old man's presence for a few minutes was an immense tonic to me. As far as I knew, everyone felt the same. Even my father, who was the most down-to-earth person I have ever known, often remarked that old Fritz always made him feel uplifted. 'There's something about that man,' he said. 'He's a mystery and a huge character.'

Looking back, I can see that Fritz was a prime example of a natural healer. He had immense compassion and love for his fellow man, and that special something that he automatically passed on to others. Old Fritz himself was extremely healthy. There are many people just like him, and we know them by the way they heal us just by their presence.

An increase in the body's levels of prana does not just maintain the balance of health, it also has a profound effect upon the psychic faculties. Prana plays an extremely important part in their manifestation and development.

During psychic development the nervous system is subjected to a lot of pressure, and as a consequence a great deal of prana is expended. Should this loss be allowed to persist, poor health may follow very quickly. Although the process of psychic development itself does not cause poor health, the subtle changes that occur in the body as a result of the powerful movement of prana can sometimes result in a noticeable deterioration in both psychological and physical health. It is therefore important to maintain regularly the levels of prana in the body while undertaking psychic development. The exercises given on p. 45 will help you to do this.

Although strictly speaking prana is neither colour nor light, both of these give substance to the waves of prana passing through the air, and therefore enhance its healing effects upon the physical body. So prana can be directed to the appropriate parts of the body with the help of colour. In fact, colour is vitally important for the maintenance of pranic circulation in both the blood and the nervous system.

Principles of light and colour

Light is simply a vibration in the ether, and colour is produced in accordance with its frequency and amplitude. The sun is continually discharging streams of vibration known as 'white light', which, when broken down into its constituent vibrations, appears as the many colours of the world in which we live.

The vibrations of colour are vitally important to both our psychological and physiological health. Too much or too little of a particular colour can disrupt our equilibrium and have a remarkable effect upon our overall well-being.

The healing properties of colour

Although a complete colour glossary is given at the end of the book, here are a few examples of the healing properties of colour and how they affect the body.

Red is traditionally a colour of high energy and is known to encourage the flow of prana to the blood. It revitalises you when you are feeling tired or run down and will encourage the healing process when you are recovering from illness.

Orange supports the immune system and has a subtle healing effect upon both the nervous system and the heart. It calms taut nerves and can be a powerful healing balm when you are suffering from anxiety or depression.

Yellow stimulates a poor appetite and aids the digestion. Sharp yellow rays have a healing effect upon the bladder, kidneys and bowel, and may be combined with blue or purple to ease inflammation.

Green has a holistic effect upon the body and is valuable when seeking to restore health after illness. Green is traditionally the colour of the heart centre and is therefore useful in the treatment of conditions affecting the heart. The green rays of healing promote serenity, calm an anxious mind and are extremely effective in the treatment of flesh wounds, burns or other inflammatory conditions. They are also useful in the treatment of emotional conditions such as bereavement.

Blue is one of the most powerful healing colours. It may be used as a tonic for the whole body and is soothing to the mind and effective in the treatment of serious health conditions. The healing rays of blue may be used in combination with any other colour, but are most effective when combined with purple.

Indigo is an extremely subtle energy and is effective upon any condition affecting the mind, which it subtly encourages to heal itself. Indigo may be combined with almost any colour, but will especially complement the soothing rays of blue.

Purple is believed to be the noblest of all the healing colours. Its powerful healing rays encourage prana to flow into the body and direct it to all the main organs. Purple rays are effective in the treatment of all cancerous conditions and also have a profound effect upon the spirit. They promote equilibrium of the body, mind and soul.

Bringing more prana into the body

When you are starting to develop your psychic faculties, it is important to consume at least eight glasses of water charged with prana each day. This not only provides your body with the necessary hydration, but also maintains the level of prana in your central nervous system. Blue, red, green and orange are the most effective colours to use for this purpose.

Water charging

To charge water with prana you will require several coloured drinking tumblers through which light can pass.

It is best to use bottled mineral water, preferably from the country in which you live, as it is likely that you will assimilate this much more easily and efficiently.

As the levels of prana in bottled water have been greatly depleted, before you start you should pour the water several times back and forth from vessel to vessel to 'liven it up'. This revitalises the water and encourages the movement of prana, making it almost sparkle with vitality.

- ◆ On the morning of your training period, pour some water into an orange tumbler and leave it on a window sill in the sunlight for at least an hour. Even if the day is quite dull, the rays of prana will still infiltrate the water. Drink this in the afternoon, preferably just before a meal. (The charged water may be stored in the refrigerator and drunk when required. The charge is maintained quite naturally for some time, so store your charged water in bottles labelled with the appropriate colours and just put them in the fridge until you need them.)

- ◆ Repeat the same process with blue-charged water and drink it as soon as you have eaten. Blue is traditionally cold and invigorating and will have a powerful effect upon the movement of prana through your body.

- ◆ It is a good idea to drink the water charged with red rays at the conclusion of your training period. Take the water with you in a bottle if you are going out to work with a group. If you are training at home, simply keep a glass of charged water by your side. The red rays will replace any loss of vitality in your blood and will restore the depleted levels of prana in your nervous system.

◆ The green-charged water should be drunk first thing the following morning, on an empty stomach. Green restores balance to the brain and nervous system and will promote equilibrium in both body and mind. Green-charged water usually helps with the disorientation some people experience after meditation or mental training. Green is the colour of nature and its rays promote harmony and balance.

These water-charging suggestions are really only to help during the initial stages of psychic development when extra vitality is needed. Once you become more experienced and are able to cope with the various physical and emotional changes that are often experienced during development, you can be guided by your intuition and common sense.

The Energy Bodies

Each of us is an extremely complex cosmic entity, a veritable network of channels through which prana flows constantly, ceaselessly maintaining mental, emotional, spiritual and physical equilibrium. In fact the human form is composed of seven bodies, each created from a finer material than the one below it, rising from the lowest and densest, the physical body, to the highest and purest, the spirit. Although these aspects of the subtle anatomy are described as 'bodies' they are in fact sheaths or vehicles of energy.

There are many variations on the concepts and terminology of the subtle bodies, but the simplest is the system described in Yogi

Ramacharaka's book *The 14 Lessons in Yogi Philosophy and Oriental Occultism*. Something is lost in the translation from Sanskrit to English, but the basic definitions are:

◆ Spirit

◆ Spiritual mind

◆ Intellect

◆ Instinctive mind

◆ The pranic body

◆ The astral body

◆ The physical body

These, of course, are open to interpretation, and are given here only as a guideline.

There is also a matrix or network of subtle wiring binding all the subtle bodies together, known as the etheric body. It is also often referred to as the fluidic body, the double, the wraith, the *Doppelgänger* or the astral man, to name but a few of the terms. It is an extremely important but separate part of the subtle anatomy.

The vibratory rate of each of the energy bodies is higher than the one below it, and although each one is separate from all the others, they all interpenetrate each other without interference.

The Chakra Network

The movement of energy through the subtle anatomy is controlled by strategically situated vortices known as *chakras*. Chakra means 'wheel' or 'circle' in Sanskrit, and these vortices are so called because of their continual wheel-like rotation. They act as transformers, modifying, controlling and distributing the energy flowing into the subtle anatomy in much the same way as electrical transformers modify electricity. The energy that flows through the chakras connects the subtle bodies to each other.

The major chakras

Although there are thousands of major and minor chakras permeating the subtle anatomy, there are seven primary vortices which are responsible for the development of individual consciousness, and these are to be found lying across the surface of the etheric body in the spinal column.

Although these main chakras are mostly invisible to the physical eye, once even the most rudimentary form of psychic ability has been developed they can be seen as circles of light measuring approximately two and a half inches in diameter and glowing dully. In a way they are like small flowers attached to a fine stem, with the number of petals increasing as they ascend the spine.

Recently, the development of a special sensitive camera combined with a bio-sensitive meter has enabled the existence of the chakras to be scientifically proven.

The Sanskrit names of the major chakras and their anatomical positions are as follows.

Sanskrit name	Anatomical location
Muladhara	Base of spine (sacral and coccygeal plexuses)
Svadisthana	Navel (urogenital system)
Manipura	Solar plexus (digestive system)
Anahata	Heart (cardiac plexus; circulatory system)
Vishudda	Throat (thyroid; superior, middle and interior cervical ganglia)
Ajna	Between the brows (pituitary body; autonomic nervous system)
Sahasrara	Crown (cerebral cortex; entire nervous system; tissues of the body)

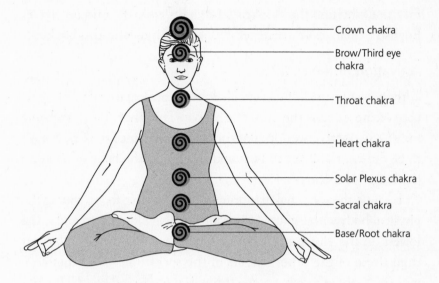

Crown chakra

Brow/Third eye chakra

Throat chakra

Heart chakra

Solar Plexus chakra

Sacral chakra

Base/Root chakra

The positions of the chakras on the body

I have chosen the Sanskrit terminology to describe the individual chakras as the actual Sanskrit words do not translate into English. Their anatomical locations (root, sacral, solar plexus, heart, throat, brow and crown) are the nearest English representations that can be found.

Although not absolutely essential, it is a good idea to fix the Sanskrit names of the chakras in your mind to facilitate a deeper understanding of them. Learning the names by rote also serves as a discipline which may be useful later on in your development. I personally found that by learning the Sanskrit terms I was able to use them as memory pegs, enabling me to recall the information to which they related with greater ease. Those who have attended my workshops over the years have also found learning the Sanskrit terminology both practical and useful.

When they are spoken correctly, the vibration of the Sanskrit words will encourage the release of the inherent properties of the chakras themselves. Of course, this is purely a matter of choice, and

49

for those who find the Sanskrit terms a little too daunting I offer an English explanation whenever necessary throughout this book.

Activation of the chakras

Although at birth all the major chakras are present, the chakra at the base of the spine is the only one active. This chakra is responsible for the instinctive workings of the body and causes the first breath to be drawn, the heart to beat and the lips of the baby to move to the breast of the mother.

Because the root chakra is primarily responsible for providing the physical body with vitality, it is traditionally coloured red and is the lowest on the vibratory spectrum. The vibrations of red are slower than those of the other colours of the spectrum, so are therefore more efficient at moving prana through the physical body. The root chakra focuses the consciousness on all bodily needs.

The root chakra controls everything for the first 12 months of a child's life, then the second chakra becomes active. A new chakra becomes active every 12 months, so it takes seven years for the entire system to become operational.

Until this age the function of the chakras is quite specific – they feed the body, mind and spirit with a constant supply of prana. The child retains a memory of all the lives he or she has lived before this one. After this, as a direct consequence of parental training, the rotation of the child's chakras gradually alters and the memory of pre-life experience is lost somewhere in the subconscious mind. However, these memories can be revived through the process of psychic development, which realigns the chakras and normalises their polarity. In this sense, psychic development is about remembering what has been long forgotten. In fact, some schools of thought refer to chakras as 'cosmic banks' and believe that all the experience of previous incarnations is contained within them. So we can see that the chakras play an extremely important part in the evolution of consciousness.

I have experienced this in my own life, and by making a detailed analysis of the changes I have been through, I have been able to calculate the whole process of my consciousness transformation. For example, I have not acquired much of the esoteric knowledge I have through learning, nor has someone else passed it on to me. It has somehow arisen from within me. This is in fact the very nature of esoteric understanding. Of course, I have read a great deal, but an awful lot of the books I read merely give substance and foundation to what I already know. It is my belief that the cosmic data stored in the chakra system is responsible for this.

If you make an analysis of your own life, you can see a cosmic influence at work on your actions, your thought processes and the decisions you ultimately make. As a child I knew someone who had very poor schooling and as a consequence could barely read or write at the age of 14. Yet he grew up to be an extremely successful poet and writer, and today is quite well known in his field. This sort of development does not come about by chance but is the natural result of chakra programming – a cosmic influence at an extremely subtle level.

From the very moment you express an interest in things of a spiritual or esoteric nature, the individual chakras begin processing the appropriate data to pass on to your subconscious mind. You will sometimes experience this transformation when you are faced with a sequence of events that you intuitively predict before they take place. You will not know *how* you know, you will just *know*. And if you look back at the saddest and most difficult periods of your life, you will begin to see some semblance of order and become aware of the pattern of transformation in your own consciousness.

During psychic development, the incredible increase in the amount of prana drawn into the body causes an acceleration in the movement of each chakra. As already mentioned, in the undeveloped person the chakras glow dully and are around two and a half inches in diameter. However, their infusion with prana causes a remarkable metamorphosis. Not only is the size of each chakra increased but the colour is also greatly enhanced, and they all become sparkling whirlpools of vitality.

Developing your chakras will enhance any latent abilities you have, but these need not necessarily be psychic abilities, as the chakras also relate to the mental abilities necessary for day-to-day work. For example, a successful police officer will use the brow chakra, which aids concentration, intuition and awareness, while a compassionate person working in a caring profession usually alternates between the heart and the solar plexus chakras, both of which are closely associated with the emotions. The heart centre is the chakra of compassion and sensitivity, and the solar plexus centre is closely associated with feelings and relationships.

RAY'S STORY

Working with the chakras transformed the life of Ray Saunders, an old friend. He had been married for 25 years when his wife decided that, as their three children were grown up with families of their own, she wanted her freedom and left to begin a new life in London. Ray couldn't cope, lost his job and then began to drink heavily. I introduced him to my chakra workshop, and although initially he found it a little hard to comprehend, one week something just 'clicked' with him and he began to find it all very interesting. I designed a very simple programme for him which worked amazingly well, and within six months he had stopped drinking completely. Today Ray runs a meditation centre in Australia and is married to Shamita, a young lady he met while visiting an ashram in India. You would not think he was the same man at all. He is more positive than ever before, with a more spiritually focused attitude than he had thought possible.

The Nadis

The chakras are connected to the endocrine glands and nervous system through an extensive system of energy channels known as *nadis*. Nadi is a Hindi word which means 'nerve'. It is along the nadis that prana flows from the chakras to the organs of the body.

The nadis are directly connected to the meridians of acupuncture. The meridians are often likened to a tree trunk and the nadis the branches.

Although there are millions of nadis, there are three primary ones. The Sanskrit names of these are *Ida nadi*, *Pingala nadi* and *Sushumna nadi*.

Pingala nadi regulates the energy passing through the right nostril and exerts control over the left side of the brain. This represents the male nature or yang principle and produces a positive polarity. In yoga it is symbolically represented by the sun and is referred to as Ha.

Ida nadi regulates the energy passing through the left nostril and exerts control over the right side of the brain. This represents the female nature or yin principle and has a negative polarity. In yoga Ida is symbolically represented by the moon and is referred to as *Tha*.

The words Ha and Tha are the origin of the word *Hatha*, which refers to the physical disciplines of yoga. Roughly translated, Hatha means 'male and female' and *Yoga* means 'union'. This illustrates the importance of balance between the masculine and feminine energies.

Sushumna nadi is the central spinal channel and directs the energy to and from the nervous system. Ida and Pingala nadis extend from the root chakra to the brow chakra and cross Sushumna in a serpentine pattern, meeting it at each chakra.

Arm pressure exercise

When the individual chakras become deficient in pranic vitality, the overall performance of the subtle energy system is affected as a consequence. This deficiency may occur for any number of reasons, ranging from dietary to environmental. Whatever the cause, you should use this exercise to examine yourself regularly, to ensure that balance and performance is fully maintained.

For this procedure you will need to enlist the help of a friend.

◆ First of all, stand up straight. Make a fist and extend the arm of your writing hand in front of you.

◆ Allow your friend to gently push your arm down, using only one hand, while you resist the pressure. The object of this is to determine your strength.

◆ Repeat the process, but this time while pressure is being applied to your writing arm, place your other hand on the lowest chakra, in the genital area.

◆ If your arm feels weaker when you touch the chakra, this indicates that the chakra's performance is impaired.

◆ Follow the procedure again, touching each of the chakras in turn. You should rest your arm for a moment before touching each chakra.

   ◆ If the lowest chakra is deficient, the physical results are lethargy, lack of drive and motivation.

   ◆ A deficiency in the second chakra is an indication of lack of understanding and compassion. It may also manifest as nervousness and irritability.

   ◆ A deficiency in the third chakra is an indication that you find it difficult to communicate your thoughts and feelings and that you may also be insecure and lack confidence.

   ◆ A deficiency in the fourth chakra is an indication that you can be jealous and possessive, and may feel unworthy in relationships.

   ◆ A deficiency in the fifth chakra indicates that your creative nature is inhibited and that you may lack self-expression.

- ◆ A deficiency in the sixth chakra indicates a lack of self-worth and the need for courage to break out of your routine. It would also suggest that you need to set yourself goals in life.
- ◆ A deficiency in the seventh chakra indicates exhaustion and indecisiveness and a lack of awareness.

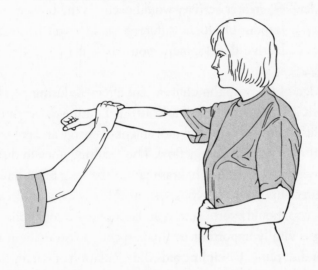

Ask a friend to press on your arm

Although a sluggish chakra system can be a long-term problem, in the majority of cases the condition normalises itself. As you work your way through the programme, you should find that the vitality levels in your chakras will be increased as your faculties begin to develop. Your chakras need to be constantly vitalised. This is a mental process of positive thinking, correct attitude and kind and loving action.

The Effect of Psychic Development on the Subtle Anatomy

Energy is constantly flowing through the nadis, maintaining mental, emotional and physical balance. As soon as you have any involvement in a training regime to expand your consciousness, there is a sudden movement of energy through your subtle anatomy, which stimulates your individual chakras, releasing their inherent qualities in line with your potential. For example, should you have a leaning towards a creative skill, then greater activity would occur in the throat chakra, whereas should you have clairvoyant tendencies, greater activity would occur in the brow centre. Each chakra is responsible for a different quality, and by undertaking their collective development you can enhance your own psychic gifts.

Knowledge of the way the chakras are affected during psychic development is vitally important, as continual misuse or overuse of psychic abilities causes a perpetual movement of energy and prevents the restoration of normal energy flow. The resulting uneven distribution of energy through the chakras may, in the long term, have a profound effect upon the nervous system. This is why, as already mentioned, you should exert caution and not overuse your abilities.

Training is vitally important in this respect, as it usually instils the need for discipline. Discipline aids the regulation of energy flow throughout the nadis and maintains the chakra balance.

Kundalini

Lying dormant at the base of the spine in the root chakra, Muladhara, is a concentration of cosmic life energy known as *kundalini*. Once awakened, it increases your spiritual knowledge and encourages mystical experience. It can be activated through specific meditation techniques, but psychic development will awaken it quite naturally.

The ancients believed kundalini to be so powerful that the very word could not be uttered, and it is usually depicted as a flaming cross or a sleeping serpent coiled three and a half times at the base of the spine. As the root chakra controls excretion and reproduction, in Tantric philosophy kundalini is sometimes associated with procreation and sexual energy.

Although it is sometimes referred to as *Prana Shakti*, kundalini is a completely different force from that of prana. Prana comes from the sun and kundalini rises from the earth; prana perpetuates life and kundalini encourages it. Prana is often referred to as the male and kundalini the female. Although the two forms of energy are distinct and separate from each other, both are controlled by the chakras and interact perfectly.

Once you engage in the strict routine of kundalini meditation, the movement of prana is redirected to the root chakra, where it arouses the 'sleeping serpent'. When kundalini is awakened it begins to move along Sushumna, the spinal nadi, igniting each chakra en route. Then, as with prana, the chakras with the most psychic potential are energised and any latent abilities can be released.

Misuse of the kundalini can cause all sorts of health problems, and in extreme cases death ensues. Some years ago now I met a young man in north London who ran a centre devoted totally to kundalini meditation. He had studied the subject in India, and he himself had the appearance of an Indian mystic. He told me of a young woman in his group who had developed kundalini to such a high degree that she was able to move solid objects telekinetically. Although he had trained her in the art of self-control, she began to ignore his warnings. Her complete lack of discipline and regard for her extraordinary ability inflated her ego so much that she left the group to start one herself. Unfortunately, she attracted the wrong type of person and found herself involved in the less spiritual side of psychic development. Although she had previously enjoyed good health and was seemingly quite strong, she died suddenly of heart failure.

It must be said that it is extremely difficult to awaken kundalini intentionally, and only the most experienced minds are able to do this. I would like to reassure you that there is absolutely no danger at all of your being affected adversely by the movement of kundalini during your holistic psychic development programme. During psychic development kundalini normally rises and falls quite naturally without causing any real harm. The example given above was an extreme case, offered only to illustrate the power of kundalini and the part it plays in the manifestation of psychic abilities.

Crystals

As crystals help to create an extremely spiritual atmosphere for someone aspiring to develop their psychic faculties, it is always useful to have a collection of them. Although there are many different kinds, my favourite stones are amethyst, rose quartz and clear quartz. Amethyst is extremely beneficial to have around. Because of its calming properties it is referred to as 'the spiritual stone'. It is pleasant to hold during meditation and is known to affect the Third Eye.

Here are the crystals that correspond to the chakras:

- ◆ Crown: Amethyst, clear quartz and diamond
- ◆ Brow: Amethyst, azurite and fluorite
- ◆ Throat: Aquamarine, lapis lazuli and turquoise
- ◆ Heart: Emerald, rose quartz and tourmaline
- ◆ Solar plexus: Aventurine quartz, yellow citrine
- ◆ Sacral: Carnelian, citrine and golden topaz
- ◆ Root: Bloodstone, hematite, tiger's eye.

Now you know the basics of the subtle energy, let's explore the mysteries of the aura – the key to all psychic phenomena. An understanding of the aura will give you a greater and more profound insight into your true psychic potential.

Discover Your Aura

Each of the bodies of our subtle anatomy radiates energy, and the combination of all this energy constitutes the aura. Everything, both animate and inanimate, has its own aura. Usually a person's aura is

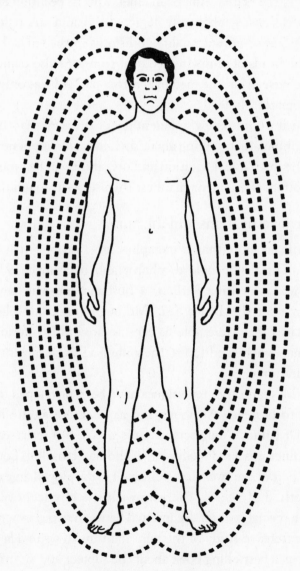

The aura of the human body

luminous and extends some three to four feet into the surrounding atmosphere, changing with every passing thought and emotion.

In ancient times mystics used their perception of the aura to gain access to a wealth of personal information about individuals. The headdress of the Native American chief, with its beautiful display of coloured feathers, symbolically depicted the aura and represented the warrior's wisdom, spirituality and status in the tribe. The halo around the heads of saints in medieval paintings also depicted the aura. Of course, what the medieval artists painted was only a small part of a greater whole.

Medieval wizards knew sufficient about the aura that they were able to manipulate it to bring about such miraculous phenomena as healing the incurable, levitation and invisibility. In fact most if not all paranormal phenomena manifest themselves through the aura.

Scientific investigations into the aura

The aura is far more than a metaphysical concept – it is a scientific fact. The first people to photograph it, around 1939, were Semyon and Valentina Kirlian, a husband-and-wife team from Krasnodar near the Black Sea. Although the crude black-and-white images they were able to capture are vastly inferior to the colour images achieved today, their method was both innovative and inspirational.

Over the years other techniques have been developed to enable the aura to be seen. Although not as effective as the Kirlians' camera, Dr Kilner's 'aura screen' gave rise to further research. Dr Walter Kilner was a radiologist at St Thomas' Hospital, London, in the early part of the twentieth century. He developed an extremely crude method of 'seeing' the aura with the physical eyes which involved a special coal-tar dye inserted between two glass screens. Dr Kilner's extensive study of the aura led him to write *The Human Atmosphere*, a bestselling book about the subject and an inspiration to others working in the field.

Scientific experiments with the aura have shown that it is greatly affected by external forces. In one experiment, a horseshoe magnet was held approximately six to eight inches from the body of a healthy person and his aura was seen to become more brilliant and alive with vitality. Energy was seen to stream from the magnet in the direction of the aura for at least 30 seconds.

The vitality of the aura may also be enhanced or weakened by the food that we eat. This is one of the reasons why a healthy diet is important to anyone endeavouring to develop their psychic abilities. Scientific observations made in Russia revealed that almost a minute after eating a heavy meal the aura of a psychic was overwhelmed by a deep shade of red and then became extremely dull and lifeless. On the other hand, after consuming a light salad followed by two glasses of water, the aura of another psychic taking part in the experiment appeared to sparkle with vitality.

The aura is also definitely affected by the company we keep. Research has shown that when a man and woman who are obviously attracted to one another stand close together, their auras become much brighter and more vibrant.

Seeing the aura

Most psychics claim to be able to see the aura, though initially they may only be able to see a small part of a greater whole, and by developing the awareness a more extensive area of the aura may become apparent. Those who have the ability to see the aura in its entirety are able to access a great store of information about the person to whom the energy field belongs.

From as far back as I can remember I have been able to see a coloured mist around people. My mother was forever shouting at me to stop squinting, as this was the way I used to bring the aura into focus. Thankfully, I no longer have to do that and can now 'see' the aura easily. Squinting is not recommended, but techniques for seeing the aura are given below. Though most people cannot see auras naturally, nearly everyone has sensed someone's aura at some time in their lives, whether they know it or not. For example, you may be sitting quietly in a theatre, waiting for the show to begin, when you are suddenly overwhelmed by a feeling of unease that makes you turn round. On doing so, you catch the eye of someone staring intently at you. This kind of experience is quite common and a prime example of 'auric sensing'.

I once knew a medium who had been blind from birth. Using her auric skills while giving a demonstration of mediumship, she was able to point directly at the person to whom a message was being given and could even tell whether it was a man or woman and what colour clothes they were wearing, even though she had never seen colour. She was quite amazing.

Health and the aura

It is probably true to say that most healers can sense the aura and will often find their hands drawn to the affected part of the body where treatment is required. They may feel intense heat, or perhaps coldness, around the troubled area.

Disease becomes apparent in the aura long before it manifests itself in the physical body, and so developing the ability to see the aura offers immense advantages to the healer.

A healthy aura almost shines with vitality and has straight radiation lines with no fragmentations. An unhealthy aura is dull and lifeless with inconsistent radiation lines and numerous fragmentations, which are indicative of poor energy flow and consequent ill health.

Although it is not ethical for a psychic to diagnose illness, knowledge of the meaning of the various colours in the aura is extremely useful. The glossary of colours at the end of the book should help you in your analysis. However, the best knowledge is that which comes to you through personal experience, and so the list of colours should be used only as a guideline.

When endeavouring to analyse someone's health through their aura, you must always observe the way the colours relate to one another. For example, blue may have a background of dark green or even brown, indicating that the vitality is restricted in some way. This may not be an indication of serious illness, but reveal simply that this part of the body is troublesome for some reason. When there is serious disease in the body the aura around the relevant area often appears dark and lifeless. Patches of grey can be apparent, particularly when cancer is present.

Remember, though, that analysis can be tricky and should always be conducted with care. Being able to see the aura is not enough to guarantee a correct interpretation of it. Many years ago now I consulted a so-called international medium of great renown, a lady with a vast following in the Spiritualist movement, who claimed to have 'auric vision'. She told me that I was in good health, and when I asked her whether there were any diseased areas in my anatomy she replied, 'None whatsoever!' I knew then that she did not have the ability she claimed, as she had not picked up on the incurable respiratory condition I have suffered from since I was three years old.

Aura experiments

Developing the ability to see the aura usually takes time and a lot of practice, but some people do become proficient very quickly. The aura is initially best seen with the peripheral vision, at least until your eyes become accustomed to the subtle vibrations. Eventually, though, you should be able to see the aura by looking directly at it, and will be able to see it in the dark as well as in the light. The following experiments will help you.

Apple seed experiment
- Remove the dark seeds from an apple (they must be dark and not white) and place them on a white piece of paper.

◆ Gaze intently at the seeds without blinking or moving your eyes even for a moment.

◆ Within seconds you should begin to see a luminous pale blue or white glow around the seeds. This glow will appear to move slowly around the seeds with a clockwise motion, and the longer you gaze at them the more clearly defined it will become.

◆ Once you are able to see the glow around the pips, fine radiation lines should also become apparent.

◆ Now place the apple seeds in an envelope and put them to one side for a day or two.

◆ After this, take a couple more seeds from a fresh apple and repeat the whole process.

◆ Pay particular attention to the vitality of the energy emanating from the seeds and notice how clearly defined the radiation lines appear. This indicates the freshness of the seeds, and in a person would represent health.

◆ Now, for comparison, place the seeds from the previous experiment about half an inch away from the fresh seeds and see the difference. The energy emanating from the old seeds should appear considerably duller. Within seconds, though, you should see an extraordinary phenomenon take place. The energy from the fresh seeds will appear to extend towards the old ones, seemingly in an effort to revitalise them.

The same phenomenon takes place when a healthy person is in the presence of an unhealthy one. Most of us have had the experience of feeling under the weather and being in the company of someone who somehow makes us feel much better. After only a short time in their company we feel full of beans. In fact, we feel full of their beans. Just like the fresh, healthy seeds, a healthy person is able to transfer energy to a depleted, unhealthy one.

Aura dowsing

As a general rule the aura at the back of the body is more extensive than at the front. However, the aura of a visually handicapped person often extends to the same distance all round, obviously to compensate for the absence of sight. It is in fact by means of the aura that you are able to negotiate your way through a darkened room.

The following experiment will help you to understand the extent of the aura. For this you will require some dowsing rods. You can make these by cutting equal lengths of wire from two coat hangers and then bending them into 'L' shapes.

For the experiment itself you will need the cooperation of a friend.

- ◆ Ask your friend to stand against a wall facing you.
- ◆ Hold the dowsing rods comfortably in front of you, one in each hand, and slowly walk towards your friend.
- ◆ When the dowsing rods cross over, stop, as this means your friend's aura has been located. Now you have a good idea of the extent of their aura at the front.
- ◆ Repeat the same process, this time with your friend facing the wall. This time the dowsing rods should cross over much sooner, as the aura at the back extends much farther than at the front.

It must be said, however, that dowsing is not everyone's forte, and so you may have to repeat the experiment several times in order to obtain consistent results.

Seeing your own aura

Here is an experiment that you can conduct from the comfort of your armchair. Make sure that the lighting in the room is fairly subdued.

- Shake your hands vigorously for about a minute, or until you can feel them tingle.
- Press the palms of your hands together in front of you, then slowly pull them apart. As you do so, stare intently between them without actually looking at them.
- Repeat the process over and over again until you can see a luminous band of light around your hands. This will probably disappear if you look directly at it. Once you have familiarised yourself with the aura around your hands, you should be able to see the same around the heads and even the bodies of a few people.

You may even like to try the same experiment with objects such as a chair, a table or even a picture on the wall. Remember, even inanimate objects have an aura, albeit at a much lower level than people and animals.

Focusing the gaze

One extremely effective method of developing auric vision is to focus your gaze on a single point to quieten your mind and deaden your optic lens. This method of 'scrying' has been used for thousands of years, and is very often integrated into meditation, where the flame of a candle is used to hold the attention.

If you wear contact lenses or glasses, remove them first.

- Place a lighted candle on a table about three feet away and as near to eye level as possible.
- Sit comfortably and fix your gaze on the tip of the flame, resisting the temptation to move your eyes away even for a moment. It is also a good idea to resist the temptation to blink, at least for as long as is comfortable.
- When tears begin to form in your eyes and you can no longer hold your gaze, very slowly close your eyes and

place the palms of your hands over them.

♦ Watch the after-image of the flame gradually appear on the empty screen of your mind and hold the image for as long as you possibly can.

♦ When the image becomes fragmented and begins to dissolve, open your eyes, return your gaze slowly to the flame and repeat the exercise.

♦ To achieve the best results, repeat this several times.

As well as stilling the mind, candle gazing also helps to develop that deeper awareness necessary for seeing the aura.

Cleansing the aura

One way in which meditation techniques can help you in your psychic development programme is in cleansing your aura.

Primarily as a discipline, the aura should be cleansed regularly. According to some yogic traditions, to achieve this salt baths should be taken and the body massaged with a soothing, perfumed oil. However, while this is beneficial to both body and mind, I personally use the mental process given here, as I find that far more is achieved with it.

♦ Sit on a straight-backed chair and still your mind as far as possible.

♦ Breathe rhythmically, making sure that you inhale and exhale evenly.

♦ When you feel quite relaxed, imagine that you can see a blue curtain of light in front of you. See it very clearly in your mind and slowly allow it to completely envelop your body.

♦ Feel the coolness of the blue light against your skin and inside your body. Hold it there for a few moments.

◆ Allow the blue light to gradually change into a red light.

◆ Feel the warmth of the red light against your skin and then inside your body. Feel yourself glowing and full of energy. Hold the feeling for a few moments.

◆ Now see the red light changing into a green light.

◆ Feel totally invigorated as the green rays infiltrate your body, mind and soul.

◆ While breathing rhythmically, maintain this feeling of invigoration for a little while longer.

◆ Finally, change the green light into a golden light.

◆ Surround your whole body with a golden glow and feel it moving in through the top of your head. Allow yourself to be totally filled with golden light, to the extent that you *become* the golden light.

◆ Maintain this feeling for a few moments longer, then relax.

Remember, this is a mental process and the results are dependent upon your ability to maintain the imagery. But if you follow the instructions carefully, positive results should be achieved almost immediately.

As with all meditative methods, it is always a good idea to conclude the aura-cleansing exercise with some rhythmic breathing.

Once you have learned to control and work with your aura, your other psychic skills will develop as a consequence. As I have already said, most if not all paranormal activity manifests itself through the aura, so the skills of clairvoyance, clairaudience and clairsentience are solely dependent upon the stability of the aura. The aura is stabilised through focusing the mind and learning to visualise – the colours of the aura can be heightened and intensified simply by stimulating them with the imagination.

Now you know a little about your psychic nature it's time for you to take the second step in your programme, and prepare yourself mentally, physically and emotionally for your psychic development.

Step **2**

Prepare Yourself for Psychic Work

Whether you have chosen to join a group or are endeavouring to develop your abilities alone, it is necessary to prepare yourself for psychic work. This is the next step in your psychic programme.

First, though, a cautionary note: should you be in the middle of an emotional crisis it would wise not to begin the programme until you feel more settled. The whole process of psychic development is dependent upon your sensitivity and emotional status. During the programme, your emotions may become somewhat disturbed. To start with, you need to be psychologically grounded with no excessive emotional baggage. Your mind needs to be well balanced in order for it to be focused, and your emotions need to be settled to enable them to cope with the psychological changes that often occur during psychic development.

Cultivating Self-awareness

Before you can prepare yourself, you have to know yourself. This is an essential part of my holistic programme. Understanding yourself means that you are better able to understand others, and whether or not you intend to use your psychic skills by giving private consultations, psychology must always play an integral part in your work.

It is not always possible to see yourself as others see you, but the following exercise will help you cultivate self-awareness.

'Seeing yourself' exercise

For this exercise you will need a notepad and pencil, a recent photograph of yourself and a comfortable chair.

The photograph is really to help you with the visualisation process. Not everyone is gifted with the ability to visualise, and so the photograph will help you establish a positive and clear image of yourself.

◆ Spend a few moments studying the photograph to fix the image of yourself in your mind. This may sound a little absurd, but once you begin the exercise you will understand why a photograph is required.

◆ Once you are quite certain that you can recall your image without any difficulty, sit comfortably in the chair and close your eyes.

◆ Mentally create a picture of yourself standing no more than an arm's length in front of you. Make the image as clear as you possibly can, just as though you were looking at another person.

◆ Make the image as lifelike as possible, and introduce some animation into the scenario. See yourself walking, moving your arms. Create an objective, vivid likeness of yourself, with facial expressions and even mannerisms. For example, do you move your arms when you walk or do they remain stiffly by your side? Are you demonstrative when you are engaged in conversation, using your hands constantly to illustrate your point? See yourself engaged in conversation, and make a mental note of everything you can see. Become totally involved, almost to the extent that you and the image of yourself are one. Resist the temptation to allow your mind to wander even for a moment. It is vitally important to take time with the analysis and to be as meticulous and honest as possible in the final assessment. This requires total detachment.

◆ It is also important to be aware of all your negative habits and all those traits and characteristics you think may annoy other people. It is quite easy to overlook your own negative traits and bad habits, particularly when they have become well established, but you need to include them to gain a complete picture of yourself. It is not the object of this exercise to initiate changes, but merely to become aware of all those things that you might like to change later on.

◆ Spend at least 15 minutes on the self-analysis process, but try not to make it a labour, as this merely defeats the object of the exercise.

◆ When you are certain that nothing more can be achieved, dissolve all the imagery in your mind and relax for a few moments with your eyes closed, replaying the analysis.

◆ Open your eyes and write as much down as you can possibly remember. It won't be possible to remember everything on the first attempt, but what you do write down will form the initial part of your self-analysis.

Remember that although one of the objects of the exercise is to make you aware of the negative aspects of your personality, it should not make you displeased with the way you look. In fact, by the end of the programme you should feel a lot happier with your appearance. This self-analysis process encourages both an internal and an external transformation. The metamorphosis comes about in a subtle yet extremely natural and positive way, and may in fact be more noticeable to others than to yourself.

If you are wondering exactly what this exercise has to do with psychic development, remember that it is an exercise in awareness, and before you can be aware of external forces you must be totally aware of yourself.

Also, psychic development initiates deep emotional changes, and if you can learn to feel comfortable with yourself, then these changes will have no adverse effect on you.

Physical Preparation

I have already told you that I use a combination of Eastern and Western techniques in my programme. In the East, psychic powers have been developed over thousands of years, particularly in India, where they are known as *Siddhis* and are attained primarily through meditation, yogic disciplines and breath control.

We will look at meditation and breath control later on, but as initial physical preparation for your psychic work I would recommend that you integrate some simple yogic exercises into your daily routine. Yoga is not only extremely effective in strengthening the physical body and encouraging suppleness, but it also eases stress and makes the mind more focused, which is a prerequisite for the whole process of psychic development. In retrospect I can now see that it was yoga which formed the basis of my own development and gave me the grounding and motivation I so badly needed. There are many books and videos available to help you get started, and you may be able to find a local class to attend.

Another important part of your preparation is to ensure that you have a healthy diet. A variety of vegetables and at least three portions of fruit a day will keep your immune system working properly. I always advocate a meat-free diet, which encourages the sensitivity of the nervous system. Should this not appeal to you, then try at least to cut out red meat.

Drink at least eight glasses of mineral water per day, and during your training period abstain from consuming alcohol or stimulating beverages such as strong coffee or tea. (For instructions on charging water with prana, see p. 45.) Whenever I have a psychic stage show I make quite certain that I have not consumed any alcohol whatsoever for two days before the show. Forty-eight hours before an important show I also take Echinacea in tincture form. This is an extract from the Echinacea flower, a remedy which has been used for thousands of years. The Echinacea boosts my immune system and alleviates fatigue. I top this up by drinking plenty of fruit juice and at least eight glasses of water a day.

Remember, my approach to psychic development is holistic, and so every aspect of your being must be considered during the process.

Mental Preparation

The process of psychic development will enhance your whole life, but in the initial stages it will be your mind which will undergo the metamorphosis, as you will be encouraged to use it in a completely new way. Psychic development produces an effect on the brain similar to that of electricity passing through a conduit, encouraging it to 'come alive'. Mental preparation is therefore of the utmost importance.

Assessing your mental skills

Answer the following questions.

1. Do you have difficulty remembering what someone has said to you?
2. Are you easily bored?
3. Are you selective about what interests you?
4. Do you find it difficult to get excited about a picturesque landscape?
5. Do your eyes wander away when a person is speaking to you?
6. Do you lose concentration when reading a book or a magazine?
7. If your concentration is poor, what do you think is the reason?

    Are you stressed and anxious?

    Do you get enough sleep?

    Do you have a healthy diet?

Make a detailed evaluation of the questions and think carefully about the answers. These things all need to be considered, as they are paramount to your development.

The importance of relaxation

A stressed and anxious mind does not perform efficiently, and so you must also take time to relax. Forcing yourself to concentrate when you are tired certainly defeats the object of the exercise. It is better to concentrate in short, consistent periods rather than force yourself to continue for long spells at a time.

Relax whenever you find the opportunity. You might like to try the following exercise.

Relaxation exercise

◆ Sit quietly in your favourite chair and close your eyes.

◆ Mentally scan your body to find the tensest parts and make a concerted effort to release the tension.

◆ Consciously allow your body to go as limp as possible.

◆ Breathe from your diaphragm rather than with your shoulders and upper chest area. The bellow effect of the diaphragm infuses the muscles and nerves with oxygen and revitalises the brain, promoting calmness and relaxation.

◆ Breathing rhythmically, mentally infuse all your muscles and nerves with vitality, beginning with your head, moving across your shoulders and concluding with your tummy, thighs and legs.

This breathing process encourages relaxation and serenity. Once you have mastered the technique you can do it almost anywhere – out shopping, for example – and even while engaged in intense dialogue.

Exploring spontaneous ideas and memories

The information you receive from the world around you is assimilated and categorised by your subconscious mind. Fragments of this information will often rise to the surface of your consciousness, appearing either as *memory* of an event that has already taken place or as an *idea* of something that you could make happen.

When this occurs, it is important to analyse it. Explore the possibilities of your memory or idea and try to discover from where it originates. Make a detailed appraisal of all the thoughts that both preceded and followed it.

This process aids the overall development of your mind, making it more efficient when faced with an arduous task. It also encourages quick thinking and opens your conscious mind to the inspirations of your subconscious.

Training the memory

Life is the constant accumulation of knowledge, the storing up of the results of experience ...

YOGI RAMACHARAKA

Improving your memory should also be part of your psychic preparation. The three primary components of memory are impression, retention and recollection. Ease of recollection depends entirely upon the strength and vividness of the first impression. It would appear that there are two different kinds of impression: those that come into the mind from external sources and those that are created by the imagination.

The following exercise will test your recall of impressions created by the imagination.

Imagery recall

◆ Working on the premise that we think in pictures and not in words, study the following list of words and allow the images they suggest to form in your mind. Look at each word and do not move on to the next one until the picture is clear and vivid in your mind.

APPLE

TRIANGLE

TELEVISION

CAR

BOTTLE

GUITAR

◆ When you have clear pictures of all the words, close the book and see how many you can recall. Do not write the words down, but draw a picture. It does not matter if you do not possess any artistic ability as long as you express the idea.

Words such as 'apple', 'triangle' and 'bottle' are not subject to style or fashion and do not alter in form, so they are easy to visualise. However, the other words may have made you hesitate because of changing styles. The primary aim, though, is not to produce a perfect representation of the object but to develop attention, concentration and recall. See how long it takes you to recall the words.

◆ Now try repeating the process with the following list. This is more extensive, but by now you should be more used to the way the exercise works.

APPLE

TRIANGLE

TELEVISION

CAR

BOTTLE

GUITAR

JAR

RUG

PENCIL

COW

CHIMNEY

TREE

CLOCK

SHIRT

BUTTON

BOAT

TIE

SQUARE

- For the next part of the exercise, write down the first letter of each word.
- Take one last look at the list.
- Close the book and, using the list of letters to help you, try to recall the list in the given order.

This is the same principle as mentally flicking through the alphabet to recall someone's name. Although quite basic, it is an effective memory aid that we all use at some time or another.

Remembering your day

This next exercise will test your recall of impressions created by external sources.

For this exercise, take a notepad and pencil and sit quietly.

- ◆ Write down everything you did today, from getting up in the morning to sitting down to do this exercise.

- ◆ Try to be as detailed as possible by retracing your steps throughout the day. Begin by mentally picturing yourself climbing out of bed. See yourself walking into the bathroom. Continue from there ...

- ◆ When recalling a day, we tend to see only fragments of what happened, but these generally suffice to help us remember. Try to piece your glimpses together by mentally replaying your day frame by frame. For example, try not to see yourself nebulously walking across a city centre through a maze of distorted images. Be as detailed as you can. Recall faces you passed. Recollect those of the newspaper-seller on the corner, the lady with the dog, the mother with the child ... In other words, slow down the whole picture. This will take some time, but a little effort will produce remarkable results, and this method of recollective imagery is a prerequisite for clairvoyance.

- ◆ Make a note of the strongest points of the imagery. Certain faces may stand out clearly in your mind. Buildings or street names might become apparent, even though you have passed them a thousand times before and never really noticed them.

On completing the exercise, take a short break, then repeat the process. You should find that other details emerge.

Try to undertake this procedure as often as possible. Spend time reviewing your days, reconstructing them and bringing clarity to the images that make up your life.

To accompany this process of analysis, you should also make an effort to pay more attention to what you see during the day.

Cultivating your imagination

The image-making area of the brain must be developed before your full psychic potential can be reached. Clairvoyance, for example, is a creative skill which requires the ability to bring images to mind without any effort.

To cultivate your image-making skills and stimulate your imagination, try the following exercise. You will need to enlist a friend's help, and will also need a children's picture book or comic magazine.

Image-making exercise

◆ Let your friend randomly select a picture from the book and, without actually telling you what it is, describe its details – colour, shape, and so on – until a whole image has been created in your mind.

◆ Now tell your friend what you think it is.

Although this is a very simple exercise, it encourages the production of images in your mind and allows the full potential of your imagination to be reached. It is especially effective if you feel you lack imagination, and will eventually produce remarkable results.

Engaging the unexpected

Our minds become accustomed to thinking in patterns, and when these are disturbed, for whatever reason, confusion often sets in. So, to develop greater mental flexibility, engage the unexpected!

The following exercise has been designed to help you think laterally, and also improve your concentration. You will need several coloured marker pens and a fairly large piece of white card.

Colour/word analysis

This psychological test aids the cultivation of the peripheral faculty, an important prerequisite when developing the psychic senses.

◆ Write down as many different colours as you can using a different felt marker for each one. For example, begin with the colour *red* using the blue marker, then *blue* using the red marker, *orange* using the yellow marker, *yellow* using the orange marker, and so on until the card is full.

◆ Try reading the words as quickly as you possibly can from beginning to end.

◆ Repeat the process a few times in an effort to improve your reading speed.

When you are quite confident that you can read all the colours in a consistent flow from beginning to end, try the next part of the exercise.

◆ This time, instead of reading out the words, call out the colours they are written in. For example, the first word is *red* and this is written in blue, so you would call out 'Blue'. The second word is *blue* and this is written in red, so you would call out 'Red', and so on.

See how quickly you can do this. At first you will probably find yourself hesitating quite a lot, but with practice your speed and consistency should improve.

Emotional Preparation

You now need to prepare yourself emotionally for your psychic work. As a general rule, avoid stress as far as you can and try not to engage in confrontational situations. This can be quite difficult, because once your mind begins to develop and your faculties sharpen, you may find yourself becoming extra sensitive and more prone to mood swings. In the initial stages this is quite normal, but things will settle down as your development progresses.

Apart from the obvious benefits to overall health, a leisurely walk in the park each day will balance your emotions as well as increasing the levels of prana in your body. Before my training programme began I used to enjoy walking through the Blackwoods close to my home. Simply being in close proximity to trees has always had a profound effect upon my whole being. They are powerful sources of energy. Pine trees are thought to release great streams of vitality, and even though for some reason I have always felt claustrophobic around them, I am also mentally stimulated by their presence.

As well as balancing your emotions through your daily walk, it is also important to get enough sleep. Insufficient sleep can leave you tense and irritable. Whenever I have a psychic stage show I always ensure that I have slept well the night before and that I am totally relaxed on the actual day of the show.

Creating sacred space

As your psychic abilities begin to unfold, so your sensitivity will also increase. Until you have completely mastered your psychic abilities and fully taken control of the way in which they are used, you will need to find a quiet area where you can sit peacefully and calm your mind when necessary.

The house in which I lived as a child was very small, and so finding somewhere to escape to was almost impossible. However, I found my ideal sanctuary, my sacred space, at the top of the stairs, where it was very quiet. I remember the ceiling there was very high, and sounds echoed so loudly that I could almost hear my own thoughts resounding from wall to wall. To me this was the perfect place to be alone. Sitting there, I could be at peace with the world. Unfortunately, I can no longer sit on the stairs, as it would look a little strange! Nonetheless, I fondly recall the sacred space of my childhood.

You too should create your own very special place, away from the stresses of your everyday life. It need not be in your home – as long as it provides you with a feeling of peace and serenity, it matters very little where it is. It might be a small corner of your garden or even a tiny area of a nearby park. It can even be purely imaginary. Should you prefer to create it this way, though, make quite sure that the imagery is consistent and that it is the same every time you enter it.

Once you have found your sacred space, mentally make it your own by imbuing it with your thoughts and feelings. Take as much time as you need to do this.

If your sacred space is not in your home, you should be able to mentally access it at any time. Wherever you have created your sanctuary, make quite certain that you have its image fixed in your mind so that you can transport yourself there whenever you need to, wherever you are.

Now you are mentally, physically and emotionally prepared, we'll start work on exercising your senses and improving your concentration and observation skills, which is the third step in your programme.

Improve Your Concentration and Observational Skills

I always instil in my students the importance of learning to control the mind by training it to be more focused. A butterfly mind is not efficient when endeavouring to process psychic impressions or images. In fact, if you find it difficult to concentrate, any clairvoyant skill you develop will never be under your control and will never reach its full potential.

Please do not think, as many people do, that if you have a butterfly mind there is nothing whatsoever you can do about it. This is simply not true. A butterfly mind is very often the result of two factors: laziness and anxiety.

When training the mind it is important to avoid all stimulating substances, such as strong coffee, tea, drugs or alcohol. Many people think that alcohol relaxes you and makes you more psychically efficient, but this is completely wrong. It is the same as driving your car while under the influence of alcohol; you may think your responses are better, but in fact they are impeded.

So, the first thing to do to improve your concentration and observation skills is to turn off and relax. Reading is an ideal way to relax while exercising concentration and imagination. Writing a story or even a piece of poetry will also cultivate the creative powers of the mind. Expressing your creative skills, whether or not you feel you have any, will be beneficial, as will exercising your senses.

Exercising the Senses

We are greatly influenced by the world in which we live and ultimately *know* this world by means of our five senses, which enable us to *see*, *touch*, *taste*, *smell* and *hear* our surroundings. However, the information we receive through our senses is minimal in terms of what there is to be known. To maximise your psychic potential, your senses must be fully developed, otherwise your skills will always be limited.

To start with, take a daily walk – in the countryside, by the sea, in your local park – making sure that you pay attention to your surroundings. Don't make excuses because the weather is not very nice – face the elements and enjoy the beauty of nature! Remember the poet's caution:

> *What is this life, if full of care,*
> *We have no time to stand and stare.*
>
> *No time to stand beneath the boughs*
> *And stare as long as sheep or cows.*

A leisurely walk either in green surroundings or by the sea exercises the senses, encourages awareness and aids the development of all the psychic faculties. It should be an integral part of your training programme. Whenever possible, take an afternoon nap too, and just allow yourself to relax.

In order to develop the senses fully, they need to be exercised both individually and collectively. The only way to do this successfully is to apply them to every area of your life – to your work, your leisure time, even while out shopping. Use all your senses as often as you can and whenever the opportunity arises.

Object analysis

One ideal way of improving your powers of perception is to examine an article very closely and endeavour to see things in it you would not normally see. For example, select an interesting object from your home, something you have had around for a long time without really taking any notice of it. It could be a glass vase with an ornate design, or even a paperweight containing swirls of coloured patterns.

Simply sit for a few minutes examining the object in your hand. Pay attention to its shape, texture, weight and even temperature. Make every effort to really look at the object as you have never looked at it before. See the different colours and the way in which each colour blends into the next. Notice the shapes of the patterns and their intricacies. Spend time analysing the object. Consider how it was made, and even who made it. Allow yourself to become totally involved in your ideas and images, and see what other feelings arise in your mind.

The whole process of analysing the object need last no longer than ten minutes, but in that ten minutes you should achieve a lot.

Most people use only the senses required to perform the task they are doing at that moment. Only a minority can hold a conversation while listening to dialogue taking place elsewhere, for example. Developing multi-tasking skills will enhance your psychic abilities.

Confusing the senses exercise

One very simple and yet effective exercise to help the development of peripheral hearing and vision is for a friend to simultaneously play two different pieces of music, perhaps using a radio and CD player, and simultaneously to present you with a selection of objects, two at a time.

With your eyes closed, make an attempt to isolate the individual pieces of music from the cacophony of sound, at the same time identifying the objects placed before you.

This may sound somewhat confusing, but that is the object of the exercise – to confuse and at the same time develop the senses. Practice does make perfect, and you will find this exercise extremely effective.

Observation

Observation involves all the senses, not just sight. As a child, one of my favourite pastimes was to sit quietly with my eyes closed and make a mental note of every sound I could hear. Little did I know then that this was the method employed by Native Americans when training the senses. I still use this very effective method in my workshops today, and find it a very useful exercise for cultivating awareness.

When you are working as a psychic, observation has to be automatic and operational at all times, rather like a supermarket surveillance camera. But the skill of observing is useful in all areas of life. A successful businessman, for example, needs to remain observant in order to assess opportunities.

Accuracy and speed are probably the two primary processes involved in effective observation. Accuracy can be fostered by meticulous attention to detail. As Leonardo da Vinci said, 'In order to acquire a true notion of the form of things, we must begin by studying the parts which compose them …'

This attention to detail was also apparent in the work of Rembrandt. In his early twenties he said that his knowledge of animals and figures was insufficient for him to draw from memory with any accuracy, and he remedied this by making meticulous observations. His careful studies of beggars and others helped him develop a keen eye for detail.

Attention to detail is also important in ensuring that your observations are both accurate *and* useful. When giving evidence to the police about a crime, for example, it is not always enough to say that the perpetrator was 'tall and stocky and had dark hair'. Numerous other details have to be considered in order for a correct identification eventually to be made.

A great deal of effort may be needed in cultivating observation. However, it will bring you the reward of far greater overall awareness.

Landmarks exercise (1)

One effective exercise for improving your powers of observation is for a friend to randomly select a route for you to walk. First of all, though, they must make a list of as many landmarks on the route as possible; for example: shop on the corner, lamp-post halfway down the street, graffiti on the gable-end, etc.

After you have concluded your walk, to put your powers of observation to the test your friend should question you about specific landmarks, making a note of all the things you have got right.

Initially, you may be surprised by how much you have failed to notice. And the more you look, the less you will see. The knack is to scan your surroundings and allow the images to register in your brain.

It's not as difficult as it sounds. Our eyes are usually very lazy, and we train them to see only specific things of interest or which represent potential danger, such as shops that sell something we want, or traffic when crossing a busy road. Sometimes we do not even recognise acquaintances. How many times have you ignored someone on a busy street and realised too late that you know them? We are all guilty of this, but training your powers of observation will help you become more alert.

Concentration

Concentration must also feature in your psychic development programme. Again, this is a skill that is useful not only in psychic work. In the commercial world you need concentration in order to recall names, faces or lists of data, for example.

If you are interested in something, your powers of observation and concentration improve automatically. When someone is advised to take up sport for health reasons, say, they often do it under protest. However, once a sport catches their imagination their level of interest often rises dramatically and they are able to concentrate when participating in it far more as a result.

Interest needs to be stimulated for attention to be sharpened. This is why recalling matters that are of no interest can prove to be an arduous task. Nonetheless, the mind *can* be trained to focus attention at all times.

Improving your concentration

While there are various techniques used specifically for the cultivation of concentration, there are none as effective as the candle scrying method given on page 66. This technique not only helps you to focus your attention, but it also has the effect of stimulating your mental image-making faculties. I always recommend candle scrying, used consistently over a long period of time, for its holistic effect upon the mind and as an aid to the precipitation of consciousness when one is endeavouring to develop the faculties.

Now for the fourth step in your programme – meditation, the most effective means of accessing higher states of consciousness and generating the energy you need for psychic work.

Step 4

Learn to Meditate

In order to prepare yourself for psychic work it is important for you to learn to be still and quieten your mind. This is far easier than it sounds, particularly if you lead a busy life and find it difficult to relax. In any case, it is impossible to turn your mind off completely. However, by concentrating steadily on one particular object or thought for a length of time, it is possible to exclude all intrusions and to become utterly focused. This is the primary principle of meditation.

Meditation is the foundation upon which all prayer is based, yet no religion has a sole claim to it. It is the tool of all great minds and the most effective means of accessing higher states of consciousness.

Although meditation has been known in the East for thousands of years and is an integral part of the educational curriculum in India, it really only infiltrated the West in the sixties, when it was introduced to us by the Maharishi Mahesh Yogi, a physicist who developed a method called Transcendental Meditation, or TM, as it has now become known. In fact the Maharishi Westernised a yogic method of meditation which involved the use of sounds, or mantras, and the principles of vibration. The TM practitioner was required to constantly repeat a power-laden syllable or series of syllables which they pledged to keep secret and sacred.

Transcendental Meditation effectively pulls the nervous system together and brings peace and serenity to the mind. Therefore it is effective in the treatment of psychological or emotional disorders. In fact there is a whole range of benefits to be gained from all forms of meditation.

The Benefits of Meditation

Meditation stabilises the emotions and promotes equilibrium of body, mind and spirit. It is invaluable in detoxing the mind and encourages mental stability and confidence.

Apart from raising the level of consciousness, it is an established medical fact that meditation also lowers blood pressure and relieves anxiety. It is recognised by the medical profession as being an effective way of combating stress and cultivating a more positive attitude to life. In fact, the holistic effects of meditation reach far beyond the physical body, making it a necessary tool for those endeavouring to cultivate the psychic faculties.

On occasions meditation can even produce transcendental experiences. In the mid-seventies I was meditating in the front room of my home. It was a beautiful autumnal afternoon and, although my mind was extremely alert, I felt very peaceful. I had gone through my usual routine of rhythmic breathing and had begun to focus my mind when I became aware of an extremely bright yellow light inside my head and an overwhelming sensation of floating. I made no attempt to open my eyes, for although I had never experienced such an unusual phenomenon before in meditation, it was not unpleasant. I then realised that I could actually see with my eyes closed and was aware of a yellow sheen across the room. Everything was extraordinarily intense, and my consciousness appeared to be moving freely of its own accord around the room. I suddenly felt turned upside down, with my face close to the Persian rug beneath me. The patterns were extremely vivid and somehow pulsated in my mind. The whole experience seemed to last for 15 minutes or so, then concluded rather abruptly, and I found myself sitting bolt upright in my chair, my mind flooded with a variety of unusual images, but experiencing a wonderful feeling of tranquillity. I had obviously had an out-of-body experience, or a separation of consciousness, a meditation experience I have never been able to repeat.

Although such intense experiences are relatively rare, many people experience the general benefits of meditation almost straight away. Before we explore meditation itself, though, it is necessary to take a look at the concept of rhythm, and the way in which it affects our breathing.

Rhythmic Breathing

Breath is life. Without it, we would die. Vitality from the air is drawn in through the breath and distributed throughout the body. Correct breathing is therefore important in maintaining the balance of vitality in the body, as well as in controlling stress levels and building up a greater resistance to infection and illness. Although this concept is only now being embraced by the Western world, it has been known by the yogic masters of the East for thousands of years.

To fully comprehend how rhythmic breathing can enhance the quality of your life, you must first explore the concepts of rhythm and vibration.

Rhythm and vibration

From the tiniest particles to the largest stars, everything is in constant vibration. Nature is never at rest. Energy is continuously changing, giving rise to a variety of forms, which give rise to other forms, and so on in infinite succession. Nothing is ever still. Chaos would result should a single atom stop vibrating.

The cosmos is filled with vibration and the rhythm of that vibration. The movement of the planets in the heavens and the ebb and flow of the tides are manifestations of this rhythm. The sunshine and rain cascading down upon us are both examples of the same law. The atoms of our bodies are as much subject to this law as is the earth in its revolution around the sun. Here, though, the mind is the controlling factor in the rhythmic process. Should our mind not be perfectly synchronised with the law of rhythm, disharmony will result.

To ensure that your mind is perfectly 'in tune' with the universal pulse, or Universal Mind as it is often called, you must first of all consider the rhythm of your breathing.

Rhythmic breathing exercise

In rhythmic breathing, each heartbeat is measured as a unit, so first the heartbeat must be assessed in order to establish the rhythm in your mind. Place your fingers on your pulse and count mentally: '1, 2, 3, 4, 5, 6', '1, 2, 3, 4, 5, 6', and so on. Everyone's breathing capacity is different, but in the initial stages you should use this basic measure of six pulse units. It may, of course, be increased as you become more proficient, but to avoid hyperventilating, or over-breathing, it is important to stick to this measure in the beginning.

When breathing rhythmically, the number of units (heartbeats) when inhaling and exhaling should always be the same, while the units of retention and held breaths should be one half that number. So, in this case:

◆ Breathe in while counting six pulse units.

◆ Hold your breath to the count of three.

◆ Breathe out to the count of six.

◆ Then hold for a count of three, and so on.

This should be repeated for five minutes – longer if it doesn't cause any discomfort. Some people find it quite comfortable and more beneficial to use counts of twelve and six. In the initial stages, though, this is not recommended, as there is always a danger of hyperventilation.

It is important to eliminate all external distractions so that your mind is perfectly focused on the rhythm of your breathing. It is also a good idea to keep your chest, neck and head as nearly in a straight line as possible, with your shoulders thrown slightly back and your hands resting lightly on your lap. Make certain that you breathe in and out evenly and that you do not in any way make it a labour.

Preparing for Meditation

Creating a sanctuary

Although it's not absolutely essential, it does help enormously to create your own little meditation sanctuary, perhaps a corner of a room where you know you will not be disturbed. This is not the same as creating your own sacred space; rather it is a sanctuary in which you can withdraw from the family and everyday stresses. It's even better if you have your own small room situated in a quiet part of the house where you can relax and 'turn off' completely from all the hustle and bustle.

It is important to eliminate all stale odours from your sanctuary, perhaps by burning some pleasant incense there prior to your meditation period. You will also need a comfortable chair with a straight back and some quiet music to listen to before your meditation actually begins. This encourages relaxation and prepares the mind for meditation.

Relaxation therapy

There is very little point in meditating when you are tense and fidgety. So before you start, it is always advisable to spend a few minutes eliminating tension from every part of your body.

Even people who think they are relaxed very often have a degree of tension in their bodies. Tension becomes well and truly established as a natural state if it is not eliminated completely. It impairs the quality of your life and makes you more susceptible to illness. So it is important to go through the following relaxation exercise at least once every day, preferably prior to your meditation period.

Relaxation exercise

♦ Lie on the floor with a cushion to support your head.

♦ Lie still for a few moments with your eyes closed, focusing your attention on your whole body.

♦ Focus your attention on your feet and gently wiggle your toes.

♦ Relax your feet and ankles and gradually become aware of all the muscles in your legs relaxing.

♦ Let go of your legs completely and relax all their muscles, nerves, tissues, cells and fibres.

♦ Relax the muscles in the abdominal area. Send a mental command to the whole lower part of your body to relax.

♦ Relax the muscles in your chest area and across your shoulders, and feel the sensation spreading down your arms to your fingertips.

♦ Try to imagine a gentle heat gradually moving all over your body, spreading to your face and neck and then moving down your spine. Feel relaxed and calm, and resist any temptation to move any part of your body.

♦ Pay particular attention to the muscles of your face and make certain that there is no tension there. Screw up your face tightly then relax to ensure that all the tension has been eliminated.

♦ Mentally scan your body to make sure that all the tension has been released, then lie there for a few moments, still and calm. Feel all the nerves in your body tingle as you sink even deeper into relaxation.

Once you have mastered the art of relaxing you should become quite adept at falling quickly into this state of serenity without going through the whole process every time.

Focusing the mind

In the initial stages of meditation a certain degree of technique and effort is necessary to focus the mind. To minimise the effort required, particularly if you have difficulty visualising, it is sometimes helpful if you use a few props to help you.

Should you be one of those people who have great difficulty quietening the mind, you will find focusing your gaze on a candle flame (see p. 66) an ideal way of preparing yourself for meditation. You can also prepare your mind by focusing on geometric shapes and designs, known as yantras and mandalas.

Yantras and mandalas

Geometric designs have long had deep mystic significance. Yantras, the geometric shapes of Hinduism, symbolically represent the chakras. Focusing on these shapes in conjunction with certain sounds known as the *bija mantras* (bija means 'semen' or 'essence') encourages the release of the chakras' inherent qualities or essence.

Another traditional focal point for contemplation in Hinduism and Buddhism is the *mandala*, which symbolises perfect peace, harmony and balance. The word mandala in Sanskrit means both 'circle' and 'centre', and the circle of the mandala is regarded as a potent and universal symbol of wholeness and an externalisation of the inner spheres of the soul. As well as being a geometric design, a mandala is also a sacred space, and can exist anywhere and take any shape or form.

A prime example of a mandala is the Chinese symbol of yin and yang, a representation of the harmony of the universe and the balance of the female and male principles, yin and yang. It is the oriental philosophy which seeks to achieve harmony with the changing nature of the world, and in so doing discover perfect peace within.

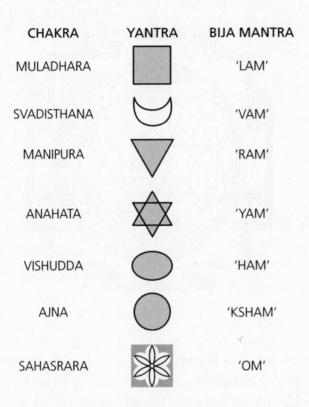

CHAKRA	YANTRA	BIJA MANTRA
MULADHARA		'LAM'
SVADISTHANA		'VAM'
MANIPURA		'RAM'
ANAHATA		'YAM'
VISHUDDA		'HAM'
AJNA		'KSHAM'
SAHASRARA		'OM'

Bija mantras and yantras

It is a good idea to make your own mandala. Create an intricate, colourful design that represents peace, harmony and wholeness to you and use it as a focal point for contemplation and meditation. Used correctly, a mandala can be quite powerful. In a way it externalises the imagination, giving it substance. Focusing on it will encourage visualisation and bring deep inner peace.

Choosing your Meditation Technique

When meditation is mentioned, most people automatically think of someone in long robes sitting cross-legged and chanting. But meditation takes many forms, and the technique that is suitable for

A classic mandala

one person may not be suitable for another. In my workshops, meditation techniques are specifically designed for each person who attends. This means that greater benefits are achieved and everyone has the opportunity to reach their full potential.

Meditation does not simply mean emptying the mind and relaxing. It is more complex than that and can involve a variety of carefully designed exercises created to suit the individual practitioner. Some people find it very difficult to remain still and quiet for any length of time, for example, while for others this presents no problems.

Finding the type of meditation that is right for you may take some time. But there is no rush. There are some ideas for you to try later in this chapter; you may even find it easier to create your own method.

Many things need to be considered when choosing your technique:

♦ Do you enjoy it?

◆ Is it a labour and uncomfortable?

◆ Does time spent meditating pass quickly or does it seem to drag?

◆ Do you feel more relaxed and yet invigorated when the meditation is over?

No matter which method you choose, always precede your meditation with some relaxation followed by a period of rhythmic breathing.

Unless you are a yoga practitioner, and therefore used to sitting cross-legged in the lotus position, you will find it more comfortable meditating while sitting on a straight-backed chair. This is known as the Egyptian posture and is the more popular of the two meditative positions.

Once you have settled on a particular form of meditation, you should devote some time to it at least once a day. Consistency is in itself a discipline and strengthens the mental processes. If you feel you can only meditate for five minutes, then five minutes is sufficient.

Try to meditate at the same time every day and be as consistent as you can, but never force yourself to meditate. This simply defeats the object of the exercise and creates anxiety. Your meditation session should always be looked upon as a pleasure, not a chore, for it is your period of escape from the stressful external world.

Meditating for Psychic Development

When meditating with the intention of developing the psychic faculties, the technique you employ should be designed to stimulate the creative areas of the brain. You should find the following meditation quite effective. Try practising it at least once a day – that is, if your time schedule permits.

Pyramid meditation

◆ Sit in a relaxed position with your hands resting lightly on your lap. In your mind see yourself standing on the golden sands of a desert. See the sun cascading down from a clear blue sky and feel the sand warm beneath your feet.

◆ In the distance you can see three pyramids silhouetted against the glare of the sun. Choose one of the pyramids and feel yourself moving across the sand towards it, without your feet even touching the sand.

◆ See yourself standing before the pyramid, a grand edifice whose apex almost pierces the blue sky.

◆ Notice that the walls of this pyramid shimmer translucently, rather like mother-of-pearl.

◆ Move closer still and feel something drawing you as if by magic through the walls.

◆ See yourself standing inside the pyramid, which appears to be filled with bright light. The floor is mosaic and cool beneath your feet. You can see light cascading down from the apex of the pyramid before breaking into a multitude of colours of all different varieties, shades and combinations. Allow your eyes to scan your surroundings, and notice the walls of the pyramid shimmering with colours of all different kinds.

◆ In the centre of the pyramid you notice a multi-faceted crystal sitting on a golden pedestal.

◆ Curiosity leads you towards the crystal, and you can see that it is this which converts the light cascading down from the apex into colour.

◆ Pass your hand slowly over the crystal and feel the sensation of electricity passing through you. Feel your whole body vibrate and fill with energy.

- Withdraw your hand from the crystal and make your way back across the mosaic floor to where you first entered the pyramid.

- Feel invigorated and full of vitality.

- Be aware of a sweet fragrance wafting over you and feel overwhelmed with a sense of peace and serenity.

- Make a mental note of all the different colours.

- Feel yourself being pulled through the wall of the pyramid and see yourself standing outside again, once more in awe of its majestic splendour.

- Feel yourself being drawn back across the sand, again without even touching it.

- See the pyramids receding into the distance and feel yourself finally settling on the sand with the warm sun cascading down from the clear blue sky.

- Breathe in deeply, and as you breathe out dissolve the scene in your mind and relax.

The experience you have with this exercise in colour will be completely different each time. This is primarily due to the development of your visualisation skills, and is an indication that the chakras in the head and throat areas are becoming activated.

Although an extremely simple visualisation exercise, this is known to be one of the most effective meditations for heightening the awareness and releasing energy into the upper three chakras. These are the ones primarily responsible for the psychic abilities involved in clairvoyance, clairaudience and clairsentience.

You may like to vary this meditation a little. The pyramid is used primarily because of its mystical and energy connotations, but you can of course use any structure with which you feel comfortable.

Recreational Meditation

Meditation need not necessarily take place while sitting comfortably in a sanctuary. On the contrary, in theory anything that elevates the mind and absorbs the consciousness is meditation.

Should you be fortunate enough to live either in the countryside or in a seaside resort, you are already in an ideal setting for recreational meditation. If you have tried meditation and have found that it just does not appeal to you, then a leisurely walk in a pleasant environment will bring many of the same benefits. Remember, though, that if the walk is effectively to take the place of meditation it must be done on a regular basis, regardless of the weather.

Walking meditation

During your walk, take time to observe the landscape and notice even the smallest details. Pay attention to the wild flowers by the roadside and the beautiful display of colour that nature has provided.

It is important not to restrict your observations. Use all your senses. Taste the air that you breathe. Become aware of the auditory experiences as well as the visual. Make a mental note of the way in which the breeze sweeps across the grass and brings movement to the trees. Should your recreational meditation involve the seaside, pay attention to the vastness of the sea and the waves lapping the shore. Breathe the sea air into your lungs and listen to the seagulls calling to each other as they swoop across the surface of the water. Allow the whole experience to pass through your mind, and for a moment feel at one with it.

The therapeutic value of this recreational meditation should not be disregarded. It may be a walk that you have taken often, but as soon as it is integrated into your 10-step programme it can become a power-filled meditation.

Meditation was referred to by the ancient mystics of India as 'the foundation of all prayer'. Meditation is in fact a tool of all great minds, and is the only means by which one can access deeper states of consciousness to become as one with the absolute while still residing in the corporeal world. Learn to meditate and you have the means to set yourself free from the limitations of stress, anxiety and a physical body.

The next step in your programme, developing your intuition, should be easily achieved now that you understand the concept of meditation. Intuition is perhaps the foundation of all other psychic skills.

Develop Your Intuition

Intuition is the fundamental principle of psychic experience. One dictionary defines it as: 'Immediate mental apprehension without reasoning. Immediate insight'. This would suggest that it is a sort of mental warning device, but it covers a far broader spectrum. Intuition is in itself a psychic skill, only in a more superficial sense.

Although everyone possesses intuition to a greater or lesser degree, it is probably only used to its fullest potential by a quarter, at most, of the people on this planet. Although it is not known exactly how it works, there is some evidence to suggest that it is more apparent in creative people. In my exploration of the subject I have found that those lacking education or who have been psychologically traumatised in some way often possess a very active intuitive faculty.

Generally speaking, women are far more intuitive than men and nearly always allow their intuition to guide them, particularly when making 'on the spot' judgements about people. My own mother possessed the uncanny ability of being able to see right through anyone who was telling lies, and always followed her hunches when making assessments of my father's business ventures. In fact, my father never made a move in business without first of all consulting my mother, whose instincts he always respected. Although he was a successful businessman, as far as I can remember he wasn't really all that intuitive. In retrospect I can now see that his success was due to my mother's intuition and not his own.

Intuition is most definitely a prerequisite of success in business; indeed, an intuitive person can never really go wrong in life. I know this statement may sound absurd to the sceptic, but anyone who exercises their intuitive ability will always be one step ahead of anyone else.

Of course, as with psychic ability, intuition can be used in any situation and for any reason, with either good or evil intent. Eventually, though, the seeds that are sown must grow, and you must take responsibility for your actions. Curses and blessings always come home to roost.

Intuition works in many ways and sometimes of its own accord. A friend of my mother's once relied on her intuition when the doctor told her that her son had no more than an acute migraine. She insisted on having a second opinion and her intuition proved to be correct. Although she had no medical knowledge whatsoever, her son was found to be suffering from meningitis. Happily, he survived – thanks to his mother's strong feelings.

As well as enabling people to sense danger, intuition can also be used to forecast future events. I once had a good friend who had a 'nose' for picking winners on the racing card. He admitted quite freely that he knew nothing whatsoever about racing, but he would always have a strong 'gut feeling' about the winner. Although his intuition was extremely effective in helping him pick winning racehorses, it didn't seem to work with anything else in his life. He was extremely accident prone and was forever having some mishap or other!

Scientific Research

In 1909 Professor Tutinsky of Moscow University made an extensive study of intuition, trying to determine why it was stronger in some people than in others. His conclusions caused uproar among his scientific colleagues, who thought that the respected professor had gone quite mad.

Tutinsky's report stated that in his opinion intuition operated independently of the five traditionally accepted senses and that there were probably five other senses, of which intuition was one. Although Tutinsky carefully avoided the word 'psychic', he did make it very clear that these other senses could not in anyway be measured with the instruments of traditional science, nor did they fall within the parameters of scientific understanding.

He went on to say that he was using intuition as an umbrella term to cover other misunderstood mental abilities, and that it was his opinion that intuition was closely associated with the imagination and that area of the brain responsible for the production of images. In fact, his experiments proved beyond doubt that the creative person was far more intuitive than the non-creative person, and he concluded that this was probably because the creative individual was more used to 'mentally previewing' events before they actually happened.

In my own study of consciousness and the human faculties, I too have found there to be a close link between imagination and intuition. It has been my opinion for quite some time that focusing the mind develops the imagination and therefore the intuition (see the previous two steps).

The Benefits of Developing Your Intuition

Developing and using your intuitive powers in a positive way can transform your whole life. It can help you to win friends and even improve your finances by giving you a deeper insight into opportunities. Intuitive consciousness somehow magnetises your whole being, making you charismatic and much more confident. It activates other mental abilities, making you more sensitive and receptive to outside influences. Concentration, confidence, creativity, assertiveness, observation, recall, perception, the ability to create new ideas and the ability to speak motivationally are all enhanced through the development of intuition.

Intuition develops quite naturally when applied to your job of work. A policeman who is good at his job, for example, nearly always uses his intuition to apprehend the perpetrator of a crime. Most doctors call upon their intuitive skills to make a diagnosis when all other means have failed.

BETTY'S STORY

Intuition can be extremely valuable in moments of crisis. In the case of Betty Bradshaw, an elderly lady whose four-year-old granddaughter went missing while they were out on a shopping trip, intuition came in very useful in helping her to find the missing child. In the grip of panic, she found her head flooding with images, and was suddenly overwhelmed by a strong sense that her granddaughter had wandered through the busy town centre towards the bus terminus. Without giving it another thought, Betty followed her intuition and was reunited with the little girl. Speaking to Betty, I could see that there was a natural awareness about her; she appeared to be extremely observant. Intuition is in fact the brain's natural radar device.

The more intuition is used, the more efficient it becomes. Meditation and various yogic practices also influence its development. The exercises that follow are derived from specific yogic exercises. They will enable you to develop your intuition, reach new mental horizons and become more positive and gain better control of your life.

Exercises to Develop your Intuition

A simple and yet extremely effective way of exercising your intuition is the walnut shell and dice game.

The walnut shell and dice game

◆ Ask a friend to place a die under one of three walnut shells (eggcups will suffice) and simply guess where it is.

- Take the exercise a little farther and have a go at guessing what number is showing on the die.

You might dismiss this method as a little childish, but it does work. Guessing the outcome of something is an extremely effective way of developing your intuition.

Intuiting images

- Ask a friend to sketch a selection of images on separate pieces of paper (make sure there are enough images to make the exercise interesting).
- Get your friend to put each individual sketch in an envelope and then mix them all up.
- Your friend should then randomly call out an image, which you should aim to find using your intuition.
- Close your eyes and visualise the image your friend has specified. See it clearly in your mind while holding your hand over the envelopes.
- Still with your eyes closed, move your hand slowly over the envelopes and see which one provokes the most reaction in you. It may be that the image you are visualising becomes more clearly defined. Allow yourself to be intuitively guided to the right envelope.

I cannot stress enough the importance of practice with this exercise. The first few attempts may fail miserably, but with determination and practice you will become more proficient and far more confident.

Landmarks exercise (2)

I have used the following exercise in my workshops for over 25 years and have found it extremely effective in the development of intuition.

You will need to enlist the cooperation of at least five other people, preferably friends who understand what you are endeavouring to achieve. The more people involved in the exercise, the more interesting it is.

◆ Your five friends should each go to different known landmarks in the area where you live. These landmarks can be anything from a monument to a cemetery, from a school to park gates. They should not be too far apart, otherwise the exercise will take up too much time.

◆ Wait approximately half an hour for your friends to reach the landmarks, then, using your intuitive skills, set about locating them.

◆ It is important to mentally create the whole area in your mind and to actually 'see' each of your friends in your mind's eye. It may not be as difficult as you imagine.

◆ It is not necessary for you to physically track down your friends. To confirm their location you could contact them by mobile phone. (This wasn't possible when I first conducted the experiment all those years ago!)

If you focus on the exercise and allow your mind a little freedom to create its own images, you may be surprised at the outcome.

Using Your Intuition

Developing your intuition can have a powerful effect on your life. As already mentioned, it can help you in your relationships and career, and in very many other ways too. Here are some examples of how you might practise using your intuition:

◆ When sitting with a group of people, try to predict who will speak first.

◆ When sitting in a doctor's waiting room, or even walking through a city centre, try to ascertain what people do for a living. You can also do this when you meet someone for the first time.

◆ Again when meeting someone for the first time, try to guess their name before you are told it.

◆ Use your powers of observation at all times.

Intuition tips

Here are some tips on how you might use your intuition in everyday life.

◆ Always respond to instinctive feelings, particularly when they forewarn you of approaching dangers.

◆ Use your imagination as much as possible, especially when attempting to find a solution to difficulties. For example, sit quietly and visualise the inherent difficulties in a situation before they actually materialise, and consciously create the results you would like to see in your mind. Always try to predict the outcome of events.

◆ Never ignore strong feelings or impressions about people you meet for the first time. First impressions are nearly always correct.

◆ When a close friend or family member, perhaps living in a different part of the world, appears continually in your thoughts, contact them as soon as you can. Never ignore such promptings, for that person may need to hear from you.

◆ Even when you are certain that you have an advantage in a confrontational situation, always listen to that small voice of intuition if it is telling you to back down.

◆ Always be spontaneous when making decisions, as this is when intuition is most effective.

Now that we've explored the mechanics of intuition you should be able to see exactly how important it is to the ultimate development of your psychic skills. In Step 6, after a review of where we've got to so far, we'll look at how you might consider which particular skills you'd like to develop further, be they clairsentience, clairvoyance, clairaudience, remote viewing or psychometry.

Develop Your Different Psychic Abilities

Before moving on, let's make an assessment of what you have already learned. Study the action points below and remind yourself of exactly where you are now, and then we'll consider where you are going to next.

◆ Take time for yourself each day and try to learn the art of relaxation.

◆ Cultivate your powers of observation and train yourself to exercise them at all times.

◆ Read as much as possible and make an effort to obtain as much knowledge as you can.

◆ If you have a butterfly mind, encourage it to be more focused.

◆ Create a comfortable meditation programme and use this religiously at least once a day.

◆ During the initial stages of development make an effort to eradicate all your bad habits. Stick to a healthy diet and take a serious look at your lifestyle.

Psychic Perception Exercises

When I was a child I used to play guessing games with myself. I would sit by the window and try to predict how many birds would settle on the roof of the house opposite, or what make or colour of car would be the first to come down the road. Although these are childish games, they do help to exercise the mind, and the more you attempt to predict the outcome of something, the more successful the results.

Some general exercises in psychic perception should now be integrated into your daily training routine. As well as training the mind and cultivating a more efficient imagination, they also stimulate activity in the brow and throat chakras and the movement of prana along the nadis. Simple exercises are nearly always the most effective. You may like to integrate the following examples into your training programme.

Finding the way in

Over the years I have come to realise that, when I am working with another person, unless I have a rapport with them little or nothing will be achieved. This first exercise will help you to gain rapport with another person and even 'read their mind'. It is perhaps more psychological than it is psychic, as it involves your powers of observation as well as your intuition, but both are important in gaining an understanding of another person.

◆ Have a partner sit opposite you.

◆ Recite ten names, integrating your partner's name into the sequence.

◆ When their name is mentioned, make a mental note of any eye or facial movement, or perhaps a shifting of bodily position.

◆ Ask your partner to think of five objects – common everyday objects, and not totally abstract or bizarre choices. They can be anything from items of furniture to types of fruit.

◆ Your partner must put the objects in a particular order and then mentally flick through them in the chosen sequence, backwards and forwards, before eventually selecting one.

- You should then randomly name a selection of objects. Your partner should listen carefully but should not say anything if their chosen object is called.
- When calling out the names of the objects, pay attention to any involuntary facial or body movements, such as you noted before, on the part of you partner, but do not allow them to see what you are doing.
- Tell your partner what object you think they selected.

The process may take some time, but with practice you will 'hit' on the correct object.

This method was favoured by Victorian theatrical mind-readers and is a training method I still use in my workshops today.

Coloured shapes exercise

For this exercise you will need several small envelopes and a variety of different-coloured cut-out shapes. Use as many shapes as you can, including circles, squares, stars, triangles, oblongs and any others you can think of. It is best to have a friend to help you with the exercise to avoid the possibility of your memory interfering with the psychic process.

- Your friend should place a shape in each envelope and then mix them all together in a box or bag.
- When this has been done, they should randomly select one of the envelopes and hold it in front of you.
- Without actually touching the envelope, concentrate on it for a few moments and try to 'see' what shape it contains. Allow your eyes to go out of focus, almost as though you were daydreaming, and imagine that the envelope is transparent and that you can see right through it.
- While fixing your out-of-focus gaze on the envelope, resist

the temptation to blink or move your eyes away even for a moment. When tears begin to form and the strain becomes too much, very slowly close your eyes and relax.

◆ Within moments, the after-image of the envelope should come into your mind. Concentrate on this image to prevent it from fading. You should begin to see a vague outline of the shape inside the envelope. The longer you are able to retain the image, the more clearly defined it will become.

In any exercise of this nature you should always respond quickly to the first impression that comes to mind. In this case, the image may change shape, causing some confusion. In only a short space of time you should find that your success rate is quite high. However, I cannot stress enough the importance of being patient and persistent. Practice does make perfect.

The box exercise

This exercise is performed in more or less the same way as the previous one. Once again working with a partner, you will need an empty box and some small items to place in it. Make quite certain that you do not know what the items are.

◆ Sit quietly for a few moments with your eyes closed, while your partner places an item in the box and closes the lid securely.

◆ The box should then be placed on a small table in front of you, at a distance of no more than an arm's length.

◆ Open your eyes and stare at the box, once again without touching it. As with the previous exercise, imagine you are staring through the box, causing your vision to go out of focus.

◆ Maintain your out-of-focus gaze for as long as you possibly

can, and when your eyes begin to strain, very slowly close
them and relax.

◆ Within moments the after-image of the box should come
   into your mind. Hold the image for as long as you possibly
   can and imagine that you can see through it. In fact, make
   the image shine as brightly as you can and, using your will,
   make it reveal its contents to you.

◆ As soon as you can see the outline of the item inside the
   box, tell your partner what you can see.

Having reviewed your daily psychic development routine, and given
you a few more exercises to integrate into your programme, we can
now consider the range of psychic abilities that you might develop.

Cultivating Your Psychic Skills

When developing your psychic abilities it must be borne in mind
that the whole process is holistic, and the psychic ability you would
most like to cultivate is not necessarily the one that will ultimately
develop. We cannot pick and choose, as the choice is not ours to
make. But the holistic approach of this programme develops the
mind to such a high degree that your strongest and most reliable
skill will develop as a consequence.

Let's take a look at the sort of abilities you might develop.

Clairsentience

Of all the psychic abilities we possess, clairsentience – sensing things
beyond the normal range – is perhaps the most natural.
Clairsentience is an inherent instinct. We all use it in sensing danger
and rely upon it when we find ourselves in the presence of someone
of whom we are unsure.

Clairsentience has a close association with intuition. Intuition is often described as a 'gut feeling' and clairsentience as a mental one. Its operation is not in any way limited by geographical space; it can be activated when molecular changes occur in the atmosphere. We have this in common with dogs, cats and other animals, which are able to detect the imminent eruption of a volcano up to 24 hours before it actually takes place. Some people experience headaches when a thunderstorm is on its way, while others simply 'know' when it is approaching. My mother used to have an upset stomach some time before a thunderstorm arrived, allowing her to accurately predict its approach.

Clairsentience also allows both animals and people to detect invisible presences. At such times we may experience a dramatic change in the temperature and feel the hairs on the back of our neck stand up. Initially we may be overwhelmed by fear, but with training we can learn to control the sensations we experience. A medium, for example, is able to translate their experiences into detailed information.

RACHAEL'S STORY

Rachael, a mother of two young children, consulted me about her experience of sensing a 'presence'. She had no knowledge of psychics or mediums, and in fact admitted that she was quite sceptical of the whole subject. She was an intelligent, well-adjusted young woman with a degree in science. Her problem was that when she was alone in the house and busying herself with her daily chores, she occasionally had the feeling that someone was watching her. She had only begun to have these strange experiences since the birth of her daughter, 18 months before, and although they did not frighten her in the least, she was curious as to what was causing them.

When I first met Rachael I could see that she was highly sensitive with mediumistic tendencies. As I didn't know what she was like before the birth of her daughter, it was difficult for me to say whether or not she had always been as sensitive, but as I explained to her, it is very common for mediumistic skills to suddenly develop after the birth of a child. The hormones play an integral part in the manifestation of such experiences. These may continue for years, although they do tend to diminish over time.

Rachael's experiences were not confined to the sensation that she was being watched; she also felt that someone was putting thoughts into her head. This phenomenon can be quite disconcerting, particularly to a young mother who just wants to look after her family. I soon concluded that it was Rachael's grandmother Jane who was watching her. Rachael told me that it was her grandmother's house, and that she had passed away six months before her little girl had been born. Happily, Rachael's experiences did subside, and she was able to put it all behind her and get on with her life.

Clairvoyance

Clairvoyance – seeing things beyond the normal range – takes many forms and can either be subjectively or objectively experienced. Subjective clairvoyance is experienced only within your own mind. With objective clairvoyance, everyone present shares the experience. Subjective clairvoyance is experienced whether your eyes are open or closed, but objective clairvoyance is experienced only when your eyes are open. A clairvoyant is usually able to experience both types.

With a subjective clairvoyant vision, images appear in your mind's eye in the same way as you see the images produced by your imagination. They can be nebulous and quite vague. However, sometimes they are so clear that they can appear as solid and substantial as external objects.

When I was a child of about five years old, I used to delight in seeing spirit forms in my peripheral vision. They always appeared like figures of light dancing to my side, but when I actually turned my head to look at them they disappeared completely. In fact, the 'corner of the eye' phenomenon, as it is called, is experienced by a lot of people. However, it is so common that most people don't even notice what they are seeing. When a spirit form appears, it is far easier to see it out of the corner of your eye than by looking directly at it. In fact, this is one of the methods I use in my workshops when training the clairvoyant faculty.

In the initial stages of the development of clairvoyance it is quite common to experience spontaneous psychic images which come and go so fast they leave you thinking it was all in your imagination. Seeing lights moving around the bedroom before going to sleep, or even small faces passing very quickly through your mind, can be typical experiences during the early stages of clairvoyance. In fact, it is not uncommon to become transfixed as you look at intricate patterns on curtains, wallpaper or perhaps the carpet, and to see these patterns transforming into the faces of unfamiliar people, animals or even landscapes or picturesque scenes. It sometimes encourages the development of clairvoyance to gaze at such intricate patterns. You may be quite amazed by some of the things you will see in them.

Even someone who has no interest in psychic matters may sometimes have these experiences and dismiss them as being no more than the products of tiredness. In fact, when you climb into bed after an exhausting day, tired yet unable to sleep because your mind is full of the day's events, that is probably when you are at your most psychic. When the body is overcome with fatigue, consciousness is in the hypnagogic state, neither awake nor asleep, allowing the mind to be at its most receptive. As a child I used to delight in trying to stay awake when I was extremely tired, as then I was able to see and hear my so-called imaginary friends.

It is also not unusual for the developing clairvoyant to sometimes experience tightness across the forehead and even migraine-like headaches. Some clairvoyants continue to experience these symptoms until they actually begin to use their skill more consistently. In their book *The Psychic Sense*, Laurence Bendit and Phoebe Payne of the Theosophical Society explain the tightness across the forehead and headaches as being the result of astral changes occurring within the pineal gland. I am not sure that I agree with this. In my opinion developing clairvoyance creates a great deal of tension in the muscles and nerves of the head. This usually persists until the clairvoyant faculty has been fully cultivated.

One lady who became an excellent clairvoyant through attending my workshops began suffering migraine headaches as a direct consequence. Although she had never suffered them before, her attacks continued for over two years before she found relief through meditation.

C. W. Leadbeater, also of the Theosophical Society, believed that before clairvoyant vision could be fully achieved an astral tube had to form within the structure of the brow chakra. In other words, the aura around the head becomes more concentrated, encouraging more movement in the brow chakra. To someone who is able to psychically 'see' the chakras, this phenomenon looks, to all intents and purposes, like a tube of subtle energy extending from the brow. This process takes place as a natural consequence of training the mind with the intention of developing clairvoyant ability.

Clairaudience

Although clairaudience is the psychic ability to 'hear' disembodied voices, these are not heard in the same way that you can hear someone actually sitting physically in front of you. Some clairaudient mediums can no doubt hear spirit voices with as much clarity as they do the voices of the physical world, but generally speaking the disembodied voices come into the mind as extraneous thoughts. They can also come as muffled sounds behind or to the side of the person receiving them. One veteran female medium I once knew described 'feeling' the voices in her solar plexus. Another elderly medium told me that it sounded as though someone were speaking to her from the adjacent room.

My own clairaudient ability works in two ways, either as a voice inside my head, usually to my left side, as I am slightly deaf in that ear, or as an extraneous thought. Though I hear the voices with my 'bad' ear, I have known other slightly deaf mediums whose clairaudience manifests itself through their 'good' ear. Why this happens I can't really say. The spirit voices I hear are mostly extremely clear, but occasionally the whole experience can be like listening to a radio that is not properly tuned in. At worst the voices can be muffled and almost incoherent; at best they come with such clarity that the owner of the voice might well be standing behind me. But of course, all clairaudient mediums are different and experience the phenomenon in different ways.

In the early stages of the development of clairaudience, the voices may not necessarily be those of the deceased. Initially, you will pick up vibrations from the worlds beyond the senses, and so the voices you hear may simply be echoes caught magnetically in the ether, rather like sounds recorded on the magnetically coated surface of a cassette tape.

Some discomfort is often experienced in the initial stages of clairaudience, and as a consequence you may experience a little depression. To counteract this, after your training period it is important to rest as much as possible. It is also helpful to discuss any worries you may have with an experienced medium or someone who is knowledgeable in such matters. Reassurance helps a great deal, but in any case such bouts of depression are transitory and should pass very quickly.

Remote Viewing

Remote viewing used to be known as 'space clairvoyance'. It allows a person to perceive things at a great distance. Today it is used for specific reasons, primarily to locate a missing person or even a murder victim. In the past it was allegedly used by the US and Soviet governments as a weapon of espionage to learn enemy secrets.

The technique is so simple that it is often used as a party piece. Anyone can do it, although it works more efficiently if a psychic skill is present.

A remote viewing experiment

◆ Ask a friend to select a location or landmark, without telling you what it is, and go there, while you sit quietly with a sketchpad and pencil.

◆ When enough time has elapsed to enable your friend to reach their location, relax and still your mind as far as possible, while your friend mentally transmits an image of their location to you.

◆ As soon as you receive any images, draw the one that makes the strongest impression on you.

Although the results of this experiment can be quite impressive, it often takes time to develop a link with the other person. Nonetheless, remote viewing is an excellent way of developing telepathic skills and quite an efficient method of cultivating clairvoyance.

In my younger years I was quite a proficient artist and used to paint landscapes from my imagination. Once I had recovered from my dark period of drug addiction, my mother encouraged me to take up oil painting again, primarily as a therapy to aid my recovery. I used to have very vivid dreams in which I would see surreal and very colourful landscapes. I was convinced that these landscapes were in another dimension, and I couldn't wait to capture them on canvas.

One recurring dream was so real that I was quite certain it possessed some deep spiritual significance. In the dream I saw the remains of an ancient cottage on the banks of a narrow river. On the other side were hills set against a clear blue sky. I made several copies of the landscape, each one showing a different season. My fascination with it became almost an obsession, and in the end I had replicated it so many times that even my mother expressed her boredom with the subject matter.

Some years later I was travelling to do a show near the Lancashire moors, and as I had arrived a little earlier than planned there was time to do some sightseeing. Stopping my car along a winding country road, I suddenly became transfixed. I couldn't believe what I could see. There was a derelict stone cottage by a narrow river wending its way from the nearby hills. This was my dream and the subject of my painting. I felt somehow overwhelmed with emotion as the feeling of déjà vu washed over me. Although I had never been to this place before, inwardly it was so familiar, and I was quite sure that there was some deeper spiritual significance to the whole experience. Although I have never thought to revisit the place, I am certain that I must have lived there in some other life and that painting the landscape from my dream helped me in my long struggle towards recovery. More than this, though, my experience was an excellent example of 'precognitive remote viewing' – remote viewing with a twist!

Psychometry

Psychometry involves gently handling an article, such as a ring or watch, whose history should be completely unknown to you, and obtaining information from it.

How does this work? We touch literally thousands of things during the course of a day and have only a superficial encounter with most of them. Nonetheless, everything with which we come into physical contact, however superficially, is impregnated with our personal energies. Should the contact persist for years, then a memory is created which can be released on contact by others. Should an item of jewellery have been worn for many years, it can impart a great deal of information about those to whom it has belonged.

Most experts in the field of the paranormal advocate psychometry as a tool to aid the concentration and encourage the development of clairvoyance. It is one of the most effective methods for the cultivation of the psychic faculties and often results in the development of mediumship skills. It must be said, however, that although sometimes you may feel as though you are picking up the thoughts and feelings of a so-called 'dead' person, psychometry does not involve mediumship. The process is purely psychic, and merely reveals the historical facts relating to the article itself. By the same token, if a psychic ever takes an article of yours and tells you something about your future, they are using other psychic abilities, not psychometry, and the article is only helping them to create a bridge, so to speak, between the past and the future.

Practising psychometry

Anyone can learn how to use psychometry, though it is not everyone's forte. For me, it does not work with small objects, only larger ones.

Psychometry is quite easy to learn. The best way to begin is to sit quietly holding a small piece of rough crystal and to make a mental note of all the images and feelings that come to you. Although the crystal will not have any historical facts associated with other people, it will have a magnetic atmosphere or aura containing the data it has stored since it began to form, probably over a million years ago. You should be able to tap into this and experience an 'at-one-ness' with the crystal's memory.

Once you have mastered the technique, you can try the same process with an item of jewellery or some other small artefact. Then you might like to try the following exercise, which involves several different items.

Psychometry exercise

- ◆ Collect items of jewellery or other small artefacts from friends or relatives. Place these on a table beside you to be randomly selected during the exercise. You will also need a writing pad and pen so that you can keep a record of the articles you have 'read' and the information gleaned.

- ◆ Sit comfortably for a few moments and still your mind in preparation.

- ◆ Randomly select one of the items from the table, then close your eyes and hold it gently in your hands. Use both hands and as many fingers as possible in the exercise to increase your receptivity.

- ◆ First of all, examine the article's weight, then its texture, its temperature and its shape. Take time with each quality and keep using both hands and as many fingers as possible.

- ◆ When you feel quite comfortable with the article, make every effort to blend with it, to merge with it, almost to the extent that you *become* the article.

- ◆ Information about the article may come to you in the form of pictures that flash through your consciousness very quickly, or you may be overwhelmed by strong feelings. Because it is quite difficult to write your impressions down while still holding the article, it is a good idea to pause every couple of minutes to make a note of them. It's also a good idea to get some feedback from your friends.

As with other exercises, a great deal of patience and determination is needed when practising psychometry. It often takes time to produce positive results, and so it should be integrated into your daily training routine.

Apart from anything else, psychometry aids concentration and is probably the most effective means of encouraging and stimulating your own psychic potential. Through the whole process of psychometry you experience all three psychic skills: clairvoyance, impressions of the mind; clairsentience, sensing vibrations from an article; and clairaudience, using your mind to 'listen' to an article.

By now you should have a fairly good idea of how psychic abilities may be developed. Let's look now at how they may be used in terms of receiving information from the spirit world through mediumship and channelling, and how to strengthen your connection with the energies of the so-called 'dead'.

Mediumship and Channelling

We live in a multi-dimensional universe in which there are worlds within worlds, rising in a gradually ascending vibratory scale from our physical world to the different realms of the spirit world. Although each of these worlds is quite separate from all the others, they all interpenetrate.

The spirit world has no geographical location – it is not a place as such, but a condition or state of being. It orbits within and around the physical atoms of this world, and its inhabitants move through and around us, totally unaware of our presence, just as most of us are unaware of theirs.

Through mediumship and channelling, however, we can access the spirit world to receive information from its inhabitants. This information may come as sound, vision or simply feelings. It is often confused and incoherent, and at worst inconsistent and vague, but at best it can be extremely accurate.

Mediumship

The skills of a medium

There are many misconceptions about what mediumship really is. Basically, a medium proves the continuity of the soul by relaying messages from the spirit world. It is not a medium's job to tell you about your future, or to help you resolve your personal problems.

Mediums are like radios or television sets – they pick up communications. We know that the air around us is filled with millions of radio and television waves, all invisible to the naked eye. It is only when they make contact with a radio or a television set that is tuned in that they manifest themselves to us as pictures and sound. Mediumship works in a similar way.

I have already said that not all clairvoyants are mediums and vice versa. A clairvoyant who possesses the ability to 'see' discarnate personalities but lacks other mediumship skills is in fact limited in the information he or she can give. That said, over the years I have worked with numerous 'psychic artists' and have always been impressed by their talents. Of all those I have seen, Ivor James (now deceased) was undoubtedly the most impressive. His drawings were lifelike and seemed to come alive on the paper. In fact, it was Ivor who first drew Tall Pine for me in a private consultation. I couldn't believe it when he held the sketch up to show me. No one else knew what Tall Pine looked like, but Ivor had drawn an exact likeness. The picture still hangs on the wall in my office today, a constant reminder that, unlike me, Tall Pine has not aged at all!

Similarly with clairsentience, a medium may be able to describe everything about a spirit person, from the colour of their eyes and hair to their height and the cause of death, and this can be so uncannily accurate that it often appears to onlookers as though the medium is actually seeing, hearing and holding a conversation with the spirit of the dead person. However, if their only gift is clairsentience then this is certainly not the case, as they are simply sensing the spirit's presence.

Many clairsentient mediums mistakenly believe that they are receiving their information clairaudiently, because it sometimes seems as if a voice is speaking to them, but true clairaudience, which involves the auditory faculties, is in fact quite rare.

As already mentioned, spirit communication can manifest itself in different ways. Sometimes a spirit voice can sound muffled, almost as though someone is speaking to you from an adjacent room. At other times it will be a clear voice at your side. Sometimes it appears as a thought passing quickly through your brain.

When developing your psychic skills it is always best to strive towards the cultivation of the whole spectrum of psychic abilities and to keep a meticulous record of everything experienced during your training programme. As I have said, you cannot choose which skills you will develop, but you can be sure that with my holistic programme you will be able to reach your full potential.

An interesting point about mediumistic skills is that they very often become apparent as a result of illness of one kind or another. Nine out of ten mediums suffer from poor health or have been through a great deal of emotional trauma in their lives. This is particularly true of those who have had mediumistic experiences from childhood. I have also known many mediums who have had their abilities awakened through drug or alcohol abuse. Once the addiction has been dealt with some internal process takes place which makes the person more sensitive, leading them to embark on a spiritual search for meaning.

During my 25 years of research into paranormal experience I have also discovered that an extremely high percentage of male mediums are either gay or have an obvious tendency to be effeminate. Please note that I said 'a high percentage', not *all* male mediums! But I will go so far as to say that mediumship is more suited to women than men. Because of their natural maternal instinct and ability to express their feelings (though there are of course exceptions), women are able to develop their skills far more easily.

If a son has a close relationship with his mother, he very often inherits her psychic abilities as well as her emotional traits. If I'm honest, I suppose I have to admit to being something of a mummy's boy myself, and it is certainly true that my mother and I had a special telepathic bond.

Working with an audience

During my investigation of mediums and psychics and the various ways in which they work, I attended Spiritualist meetings and theatre demonstrations. What I found very interesting was the different ways in which mediums presented their skills to an audience – and even more interesting was how the audiences responded. I could see that presentation was everything, and when it was combined with a warm and friendly personality the audience responded in a more positive and lively way. I realised that regardless of how accurate a medium's information appeared to be, if their personality lacked vitality then the audience would be bored and the responses negative. In fact, once the attention of the audience is lost, contact with the spirit world is usually broken.

Although at the beginning of my career it was not my intention to demonstrate my psychic abilities publicly, it soon became quite clear that this was the route I was going to take. However, I had no intention of working in the same way as other mediums, and was determined to create my own inimitable style. Although I possess the gifts of clairvoyance and clairsentience, I work predominantly with clairaudience. Initially, I had no idea how this would work in front of an audience, and decided that the only way to find out was to put it to the test. I must admit that in the early stages I found it very difficult to focus my psychic abilities while at the same time maintaining the audience's attention. I then realised that I somehow had to cultivate a theatrical persona and learn to project this to the audience. The importance of this came home to me when I worked in Brussels at a corporate event. I had to work with an interpreter, and I quickly realised that quite a lot was lost in translation. This was probably one of the most trying experiences I have ever had in my whole career as a stage psychic.

Generally speaking audiences today are very receptive. Interest in the paranormal, and in mediumship in particular, has greatly increased over the past few years, primarily, I am sure, because of the coverage the subject is now given on television. Over the last two years I have noticed an incredible change in theatre audiences.

Where formerly they were made up predominantly of women, today there is a balanced mixture of men and women. There is even great interest in places where you would not expect it. Recently I did two separate television programmes during which I had to demonstrate my psychic skills to predominantly Catholic audiences in Milan and Malta. I must admit that on both occasions I expected great resistance, but I was completely wrong. In Malta, particularly, the response from the audience was phenomenal.

Should you have aspirations towards demonstrating your psychic skills in theatres, then it is important to develop an original, entertaining style. Remember, those who attend psychic theatre shows usually have no idea of what to expect. So it is important to avoid religious or Spiritualist terminology and speak to the audience in plain, simple language. Although I would suggest that you see as many mediums and psychics at work as possible, avoid copying their styles. Cultivate a pleasant style of your own, and become known for your singular qualities.

Getting the message across

I am often asked why spirit voices can't give more detailed information about themselves. The simple answer to this is that they very often do! Sometimes when I am working in a theatre they give their first and second names and the address they used to live at. The information is often quite specific, but it all depends on the overall atmosphere at the time of the communication and how the audience responds.

It is also important to remember that communication with the spirit world is experimental at the best of times. Just as mediums are always striving to perfect their skills, so spirit people are always seeking more effective ways of communicating.

In fact, the process of communication is far more difficult than we may initially appreciate. Very often the medium receives the information from an intermediary, a spirit guide, to whom it is passed on by the communicating spirit, and the whole process can be extremely complex.

Remember too that a medium is like a radio or television set, and if no signal is broadcast neither sound nor pictures will be received. A medium is totally at the mercy of the spirit communicators, and if they choose *not* to communicate then there is nothing whatsoever the medium can do. No matter how good or well known the medium is, they do not have the power to call the spirits back at will.

Dealing with difficult cases

Some people also have the misconception that when a person passes over they suddenly become an angelic being. This is far from the truth. Death does not bring about an immediate transformation in character, but is rather a continuation of the life previously lived, only in a more transcendental sense. Just as the physical world is solid and substantial to you, so the spirit world is solid and substantial to those who live in it, and their learning process continues there.

Usually the spirit communicators who come forward are vetted by the medium's spiritual guides, and the messages they wish to convey are monitored very carefully. Occasionally, though, there are exceptions. Over the years I've sometimes been put on the spot when delivering messages during one of my stage shows. Some years ago now I had already been working for 20 minutes when I heard a spirit voice saying, 'Please go to my wife, Margaret, sitting in the front row in a red coat.' When I looked there were in fact three women in red coats. Walking to the edge of the stage, I asked, 'Who is Margaret?' One of the women raised a hand. The voice continued, 'Tell her Peter's here!'

I glanced at the woman and said, 'Peter's here!' She immediately began to sob uncontrollably. 'Oh my God!' she cried.

Her friend placed a consoling hand over hers and explained, 'He's only been dead two weeks!'

I was pleased that I had been able to relay this message, thinking that it would bring the woman some comfort. She continued sobbing, and I waited for her husband to say something further. Suddenly his voice boomed inside my head: 'I don't know what she's crying for – she's a cow! She made my life a misery and I just want her to know that when she comes over I won't be waiting for her. I'll be with my first wife, Barbara.'

I was speechless as I looked at the distraught woman. Then I knew what I must do. Looking warmly at her, I said softly, 'Peter just wants you to know that he's all right and that he loves you very much!' I felt guilty, but knew that I'd done the right thing.

Sometimes a spirit communicator is quite obscene, and shouts nothing but expletives in my ear. This can usually happen only when the offending spirit has such a strong character that they have somehow managed to slip through my own 'spirit security', so to speak. Dealing with this sort of communication is quite difficult and sometimes leaves me feeling extremely tired.

These sorts of communication are not common, though they do happen from time to time. Generally speaking it is the spirit world's desire simply to prove the continuity of the soul beyond death, and no more. In any event, it is always best if disagreements and relationship problems are sorted out in this life!

Should something similar ever happen to you, you must not in any way allow yourself to be fazed, but simply assert yourself mentally. Be disciplined, and discharge the unruly spirit characters forcibly from your mind.

Developing mediumship skills

I am often asked about the most effective way of developing mediumship skills. Apart from the mind training I have been describing so far, the best way is to give private consultations, to friends initially, and then in due course to people you do not know. At first names and descriptions may come to you spontaneously, seemingly from nowhere, almost as though you were making them up. You probably will not see or hear anything, and initially you may not even sense anything. But as long as the response to the information you offer is positive, in the early stages it does not really matter how the information is obtained. The development of mediumistic abilities is very often quite subtle, and yet with use they may blossom quickly. Try not to do too much initially – the result may be that you end up achieving little.

It will help you to watch as many mediums at work as possible, but do exercise a certain amount of caution. Working as a medium requires no special licence or certification, and sadly not all mediums are genuine, even those who are able to produce seemingly positive results and have a following.

When I started investigating psychic phenomena I kept a meticulous record of all the information that had been given to me by mediums, and I can honestly say that of all those I consulted I had satisfactory evidence of survival only from four of them. Sadly, all four are now deceased, but they had a great influence on my work today.

When I was running the Thought Workshop in 1989, I was approached by David, an 18-year-old man from Stockport who had an incredible psychic skill: he could read minds. I couldn't fathom it out, and I must admit he made me feel uncomfortable. He attended my workshops for six months, and during that time became much calmer and far more focused. He did have mediumship tendencies, but I was not totally convinced by his skill as a mind-reader.

Eventually he confided that he had learned his mind-reading skills from his father, a Russian Jew who had been interned by the Nazis during the Second World War and had become proficient at the art of reading facial language. So David would 'read minds' by making a detailed analysis of facial movements, particularly blinking. Although this technique is widely known today, I have never seen anyone demonstrate it quite as skilfully as he did. He now lives in America, and is probably on his way to making his second million! The point of this story is to underline the fact that not all mediums have genuine psychic skills. It behoves you to be vigilant and exercise great caution. When seeking a medium to consult, personal recommendation is always best.

The seagull exercise

If you are developing your skills within a group and would like to find out which of you is the most psychically receptive – a pre-requisite for mediumistic development – you might like to try this exercise.

- ◆ The person in charge of the group should write the word 'seagull' on several small pieces of paper. These should be folded and placed in a bag. It is important that the other members of the group do not know that the same word is written on every piece of paper.

- ◆ One member should volunteer to be the 'receiver'. This person should be seated with their back to the group, who should be seated in rows.

- ◆ Once everything has been set up, everyone except the receiver should take a piece of paper from the bag. The group should be told that all the words are different, and that they should keep their word secret, taking care not to show it to anyone.

- ◆ Working on the premise that thoughts are living things, the group should be instructed to mentally transmit their words to the receiver, who should remain passive with his or her eyes closed. The transmitters can either visualise a seagull flying towards the receiver or mentally chant the word, whichever comes easier.

- ◆ During transmission either word or picture, as appropriate, should be sent in a consistently rhythmical manner until the leader calls the conclusion of the exercise, which should continue for at least ten minutes, or until results are achieved.

- ◆ The receiver should call out all the images he or she has mentally received. The object of the exercise is for the group to establish a strong telepathic link with the receiver. Although the members are unaware that they are sending the same word, their combined energies should succeed in transmitting 'seagull' to the receiver's mind. The results are usually impressive – the receiver nearly always sees water and sky, and eventually a seagull swooping across the surface of the water.

The word 'seagull' can only be used once, for obvious reasons, but the same exercise may be performed using different words, as the group originally thought was the case. Mediumship is primarily based on telepathy, that is mind-to-mind communication. So the person who is most receptive probably possesses the greatest potential for mediumistic development, having a mind that is able to receive images transmitted to it by other minds.

Trance mediumship

Trance mediumship is when a medium enters a trance-like state after appearing to have momentarily fallen asleep. They will then begin to speak in a voice very different from their own and will nearly always show signs of a very different personality. I have been amazed to hear a female medium speak with the deep, resonating voice of an elderly man. These were words of profound wisdom, far beyond the intellectual understanding of the diminutive young woman. What is happening is that while 'asleep', so to speak, the mind of the medium is somehow interacting with the mind of a discarnate entity. The trance state takes years of dedication to develop.

There are various levels of trance mediumship, ranging from the over-shadowed state to the deep unconscious state. In the over-shadowed state, the medium is aware of what is going on around them; in a deep trance they are completely oblivious to the outside world and to all intents and purposes asleep.

Incidents of trance mediumship have been recorded throughout history. The famous prophet Nostradamus used to imbibe a herbal narcotic to encourage a trance-like state and transcend the barriers of time. The most famous of all trance mediums was Edgar Cayce, also known as 'the sleeping prophet' because of his predictions about the future uttered while he was in a deep trance. Today, however, trance mediumship is only really demonstrated in Spiritualist churches, and even there it is rarely seen.

In the early days of my work as a medium I used to become over-shadowed before eventually falling into a light trance. During the time I was in the trance I would expound philosophical teachings that were completely unknown to me. Each time I went through this process I felt uplifted, though I was completely oblivious to what was taking place.

It wasn't until I was invited by the Greater World Christian Spiritualist Association to speak at their anniversary rally at Leeds Town Hall that I came to realise the full potential of my trance-state addresses. After the event I was able to listen to the recording of what I had said, and was quite amazed at the content. Although I had attributed these teachings to Tall Pine, the style of the language was not that of a plainsman. A university linguistics expert confirmed that it was the language of Victorian England. It was shortly after that event that I learned from Tall Pine that there were in fact two nineteenth-century philosophers who were working closely with me. I wanted to know more.

In fact, during my trance-state periods I sometimes became conscious of a young man attired in Victorian garb, with thick dark hair and a moustache. I had no idea who he was – or why, for that matter, I could see him. It wasn't until some years later that an elderly friend of my Aunt Louise gave me a very old and tatty book. It was *The Treasure of the Humble* by Maurice Maeterlinck, and had the inscription 'To Tall Pine'. I opened the first page and, to my great surprise, there was the young man I had seen. It was the author, Maurice Maeterlinck. Though he was Belgian, the process of thought transference transcends the limitations of language, especially during the phenomenon of trance or inspirational speaking, and that is how he had been able to pass on his teachings. In any case, Maeterlinck spoke fluent English and had spent several years in England. He was also extremely conversant with mediumistic processes, and would therefore have experienced no problems whatsoever in passing on his thoughts and ideas to me.

My exploration of mediumship over the past 25 years has led me to conclude, however, that although the majority of trance mediums are quite sincere, only a very small minority are truly in trance.

Nevertheless, remarkable events can occur. In the early days, when I was a young man searching for answers, I was fortunate to sit with a small group led by an elderly medium from Wales. Madame Tickel was in her early nineties and extremely frail – until, that is, she entered a deep trance state. I witnessed various personalities transform her face as she worked with first one spirit entity and then another. She spoke to me at length and allowed a Victorian doctor to consult me. 'You have inflammation of the bronchi,' he said to me. 'You have suffered with this since you were a child.' In fact, the respiratory condition bronchiectasis was originally known as inflammation of the bronchi. At this time no one there knew that I suffered from it, least of all the frail little medium, whom I had never met before. She was quite genuine and an inspiration to me, but unfortunately trance mediums of such a calibre are few and far between.

Indeed, unless the controlling spirit entity is able to expound knowledge that is beyond the medium's own intellectual level and understanding, then as far as I am concerned there is absolutely no point whatsoever to the whole process.

Today a more up-to-date version of trance has become fashionable, and this is what we refer to as channelling.

Channelling

Channelling is one of those phenomena that has infiltrated from America. It is really only another form of trance mediumship, with consciousness focused perhaps in a slightly different way. Today it is possible to attend seminars dedicated exclusively to learning how to channel. These seminars usually include sections on 'contacting the higher self' and how to cultivate a stronger and more profound relationship with angelic forces.

Should channelling be your primary interest, you can develop your abilities easily through this programme. My holistic approach will ensure the realisation of your full potential; all you need do is focus your attention on making your mind still so that you are able to reach the all-important higher state. This may be safely achieved through specific meditation techniques (see below, and also Step 4), and by taking what you find useful in this programme and adapting it you can devise your own technique.

Learning to channel

Your approach to the whole concept of channelling is paramount. I always ask my students to lay aside any preconceived ideas and start afresh. In the development of such a skill, the mind is of primary importance, and what takes place inside your head is a purely subjective process to which you alone are a party. Honesty should be paramount, not only to others but also to yourself.

Although there are conflicting theories about whether or not you should train alone, as long as you have no history of psychological illness you will find the following exercise beneficial.

Step 1: the transfer of consciousness

◆ You must first of all learn to focus your mind and become accustomed to silence.

◆ Find yourself a quiet corner and relax in a comfortable chair. Make sure that you are not too tired. This will defeat the object by encouraging sleep.

◆ Make sure that your chest, neck and head are as nearly in a straight line as possible, your shoulders thrown slightly back and your hands resting lightly on your lap.

◆ Breathe rhythmically (see p. 93), and when you breathe in say to yourself 'I breathe in' and when you breathe out say 'I breathe out', and so on. Make quite certain that there is a nice steady rhythm to your breathing. Continue breathing in this way for approximately ten minutes.

◆ Allow yourself to become totally relaxed by mentally scanning your body very slowly, soothing away all the tension from the muscles, tissues, nerves and cells.

◆ Feel overwhelmed by a sense of peace, and see yourself being in touch with everything and at one with everything. See everything as one, and your soul, whatever you conceive your soul to be, as an integral part of that oneness.

◆ See yourself as being independent of the body that you temporarily inhabit and feel that you can leave it at will, though knowing full well that you must return to it when the process is concluded.

◆ Imagine that there are streams of intense white light streaming in through the top of your head, and see that white light filling your whole being.

◆ It is important to maintain this imagery for as long as possible, and feel as though you are receiving an incredibly powerful cosmic force.

◆ Silently send out a request for guidance, enlightenment and inspiration, and ask all those endeavouring to guide you towards the perpetual light to raise your consciousness towards divine inspiration.

◆ Remain in this state of consciousness for a further five minutes, longer if you feel comfortable, and then conclude the whole process with some further rhythmic breathing, and relax.

To achieve positive results this technique of transference of consciousness should be practised regularly for two to four months. Results will be extremely subtle, and indeed may only be measured in terms of the time that passes by unnoticed. In fact, you will lose all track of time, and the more you persist with the exercise the deeper the transference you will achieve.

Before you tackle the next stage, it is a good idea to have a notepad and pen by your side so that you can keep a meticulous record of your experiences.

Step 2: observations

◆ Spend a few minutes preparing your mind. Sit in quiet contemplation and send out a mental request for spiritual guidance and protection. Be positive and make the request an affirmation, a declaration of your intentions to those higher minds guiding you.

◆ Allow your mind to reach for the highest conceivable source of light and let yourself merge with it.

◆ This time exercise your powers of observation, and make a mental note of every minute detail – sensations, colours and even fragrances. Write it all down immediately so that you have a record of your achievements and can check how you have progressed.

♦ As before, conclude the process with some further rhythmic breathing and then relax.

Each time you carry out the exercise, do so with a different intention. You will find the results quite interesting. Only when you have mastered the technique will you be able to collate everything you have experienced into one final image.

Over a period of time you will gradually become conscious of the spirit beings who are guiding you. The more dedicated and determined you are, the stronger and more profound your relationship with them will become. (For more about spirit guides, see the Afterword.)

It must be said, though, that only so much can be achieved alone. When you feel that the time is right, sit with someone with whom you feel comfortable and in whom you have complete confidence. Your partner will be able to keep a note of your achievements, and will help to make each exercise much more interesting.

By now you should have a good idea of what is involved in mediumship and channelling. Let's go on to look at how you can use different tools to help you divine the future. These will include tea leaves, the crystal ball, the black mirror, candle scrying, palmistry, the Tarot, runes, astrology, dowsing and my very own method of psychic handwriting analysis.

Step **8**

Working with Divination Tools

From time immemorial people have used divinatory tools to foretell the future, and although some of these methods have long since been abandoned, many are still in use today. These range from tasseomancy, the art of divining with tea leaves, to seeing the future in a crystal ball.

Although many of these tools are extremely effective in cultivating the psychic faculties, in the early stages of psychic development it is not always wise to depend upon them too much, unless of course you intend to always use them in your work.

Very early in my investigation into psychic phenomena I realised that you have to adapt your methods to what you are seeking to achieve. For example, very little can be accomplished in a consultation with a Tarot-reader when you have lost someone and are seeking evidence of their survival. Although I have seen some mediums using Tarot cards, generally speaking Tarot-readers are not mediums. Furthermore, unless a Tarot-reader possesses at least rudimentary psychic ability, the chances of them being able to see accurately into your future are in fact very slim. Although most of the Tarot-readers I consulted did possess psychic abilities, there is a minority whose skills are confined to analysing the symbolism of the cards. Although this process can take years of study, in the end it does not make the reader psychic!

When choosing a divinatory tool it is always a good idea to be guided by your intuition. But here are a few of the traditional ways.

Tasseomancy

Tasseomancy, or divining with tea leaves, involves the observation of random patterns and shapes created by the tea leaves left in a cup or bowl after the tea has been drunk. It is believed to have developed in China more than 2,000 years ago. Because of the stick-like nature of Chinese tea, it formed hieroglyphic shapes in the cup deemed to have deep symbolic significance. In India, where the tea was leafier, pictures and symbols often appeared in the cup, and these were used in conjunction with astrology to predict the specific times of future events. Tasseomancy was introduced into Europe as recently as the eighteenth century, primarily because that was when the practice of tea-drinking was introduced from the East.

Today reading tea leaves tends to be associated exclusively with the fireside fortune-teller, or the little old lady sitting round the table with friends, and is perhaps looked upon rather cynically. In Victorian times, however, it was treated very seriously.

Some years ago I used to consult an elderly lady who, although she knew nothing whatsoever about me, made extremely accurate predictions based on a reading of tea leaves. Although I was ridiculed by some of my friends for visiting her, she told me exactly what I would be doing today.

While many diviners simply use the tea leaves as a focal point to encourage the processing of images in their own mind, some of the more ancient systems require a study of the different shapes made by the leaves. For example, if the tea leaves form the shape of a ship's anchor and a seagull, they are informing the reader that a journey overseas is to be made. Or they might show the shape of a cross, indicating a possible death. As the shapes created by the tea leaves are in many cases self-explanatory, this method of tasseomancy requires little or no psychic skill, and is perhaps the easiest method to use. However, as residual tea leaves do not always create any apparent shapes at the bottom of the cup, it is more effective to use the subjective image-making faculty of your own mind.

Scrying

Scrying is simply the process of 'deadening' the optic lens to encourage the mind to be more inwardly focused. This has been practised for thousands of years by mystics from religious cultures all over the world, and in many countries is still used today as a means of prophesying the future.

I have personally used scrying for many years, and find it both fascinating and extremely accurate. Even a simple glass of water can be used as a focal point for scrying. Some of the many other ways of doing it are given below.

The crystal ball

There is really no more effective way of using clairvoyant vision to glimpse the future than crystal scrying. It has been practised for thousands of years, and there is evidence that it was even used by the ancient Egyptians to see into the future. There is something about a crystal sphere that is hypnotic and almost magical.

I inherited an old crystal ball from an elderly family member who used it herself to glean information about the future. In the initial stages of my own development, I used it as a means of focusing my consciousness and making my mind still. I still use it occasionally today when I am seeking answers to specific questions. Although I don't really need to use such an implement, it does produce clearly defined images which require little or no interpretation.

Crystal gazing is extremely easy, though it requires some patience to achieve results. Although the images appear to be in the crystal ball itself, the process is totally subjective and takes place in your mind. Gazing at the ball simply deadens your optic lens and eliminates all distractions. This encourages images to appear in your mind, and it is there that the future can be glimpsed.

The object of the exercise is to achieve a voluntary dissociation of consciousness, so that your mind can become detached from the outward world and can wander freely through inner space and time.

It may not be easy to still your mind – that peaceful room can become a cacophony of noise and even the clock's ticking can seem impossibly loud the more you concentrate – but a quiet mind is of paramount importance in scrying. Trying to scry with an unsettled mind is like trying to see the bottom of a rock pool when you've disturbed the sand. The sand will only settle again when the surface of the water is still. In the same way an unstill mind will obscure the images you are trying to generate.

Practising crystal gazing

You will need a crystal ball for this exercise. These can be purchased in any new age or crystal shop. Although there are numerous ways of using the crystal ball, I find the best results are obtained by placing it on black velvet in subdued lighting. Although light reflections cannot be completely eliminated, you must learn to ignore them as much as possible and allow your gaze to rest comfortably upon the surface of the crystal.

A great deal of patience is required, so be prepared to expect some disappointment in the initial stages. It can take longer for some people to get results than for others. Because of the danger of optical fatigue, do not devote any longer than ten minutes to the exercise at first.

◆ Place the crystal ball on a table at arm's length. Sit comfortably and still your mind.

◆ Turn your gaze gently to the crystal ball and just stare into it. Resist the temptation to blink or move your eyes away from the crystal even for a moment.

◆ When tears begin to form and you can no longer continue to stare, close your eyes and place the palms of your hands over them. Within moments the after-image of the crystal ball will appear. Hold the image there for as long as you can, and when it begins to fade open your eyes and return your gaze to the crystal.

◆ Repeat this process at least five times and then relax.

◆ Take a break for five minutes before returning to the exercise.

◆ Sit quietly and gently turn your gaze once more to the crystal, this time allowing yourself to blink when necessary. It is sometimes a good idea to stare at a selected point on the surface of the crystal and to maintain this stare all through the exercise.

◆ Eventually you should see a shadow descend to cover the crystal completely. This may remain for some time, so be patient.

◆ Finally the shadow should rise and the crystal will appear to have an effervescent glow. This too will eventually disappear, hopefully to reveal fleeting images, such as landscapes, faces, colours or different shapes. In the initial stages these images will have no significance at all – they are merely things surfacing from deep within your subconscious mind – but ultimately crystal gazing will reveal many significant images to you.

When I first began to use the crystal seriously as a means of focusing my mind, I found it quite difficult. Nothing happened for quite a long time. My elderly aunt had given me some tips, but I wanted results, and I wanted them right away. I was beginning to get disheartened with the whole process.

One very cold and blustery night I had settled down in the front room to begin my period of scrying. The lighting was subdued and I had positioned the crystal on its wooden pedestal on a black velvet cloth in the centre of the table. I had followed the same procedure every night for the past 12 months, and now I was beginning to get really fed up with the whole thing.

Then, as I gazed at the crystal ball, it began to change. It had a green glow and appeared to be effervescent. The whole crystal pulsated and then became very bright and clear. It seemed to go out of focus and appeared to move on its pivot. I felt a rush of excitement as the crystal somehow came alive. At that point a shadow descended, covering the crystal completely. It seemed to remain in darkness for ever, and just as I was about to abandon the whole procedure the shadow dissolved, revealing beautiful landscapes deep within the crystal. One after another they flashed by, and I was mesmerised by the whole display. Suddenly everything went dull for a moment. Then the brightness intensified and I began to see faces smiling out at me, one after another, vibrant and alive and encapsulated in the crystal sphere. At that time the faces meant nothing to me. Suddenly the display came to an end, leaving the room in darkness.

That was 30 years ago, and now all but one of those faces has become known to me. The first was a guy called Phil, who became one of my closest friends and who worked with me for some years. Another was the writer and mystic Maurice Maeterlinck, who I now believe is guiding me in my work. There was also Sylvia Alexio, the elderly medium who helped me a great deal later on, my son Ben, as he is now at the age of 19, my present wife, and various other people who are significant to me. They all first came to me in the crystal 30 years ago. The question I asked then and still ask today is *why?*

Giving a reading with the crystal ball
Once you feel quite comfortable using the crystal ball, and have become quite proficient at 'seeing' with it, you might like to try giving a reading to another person.

- ◆ Ask someone to hold the crystal ball for a few moments, or place it against their forehead.

- ◆ Take the crystal from them and return it to its pedestal or black velvet. Relax, fix your gaze on the surface of the crystal and simply scry as you have done previously.

- ◆ This time the images and shapes should have some significance and will probably (though not inevitably) relate to your sitter.

As with everything, practice makes perfect. The more you use the crystal ball, the clearer the images will be.

The concave black mirror

A similar divinatory method is the concave 'black mirror'. This is usually made of black onyx, although a bowl painted black will suffice. Although the procedure is the same as for the crystal ball, some people find this method of divination works better for them. Because of its dark appearance, the mirror is extremely effective in encouraging the production of images in the mind.

Another method is to drop some black ink into a bowl or glass of water. This can produce equally good results.

Candle scrying

Although I discussed candle gazing earlier, as a means of improving concentration and stilling the mind, it is worth exploring again from a different perspective.

Candle gazing is a very effective method of cultivating the skill of clairvoyance. In yoga the exercise is referred to as *Tratak*, and involves gazing at the flame without blinking. As a divinatory tool, it produces some remarkable results, and for some people is the easiest scrying method to use.

Practising candle gazing

- To create the right atmosphere, burn some pleasant incense and, if you like, play some meditative music.
- Place a lighted candle as near to eye level as possible, no more than a few feet away from you.
- Turn off the lights, sit comfortably in front of the candle and simply gaze at the tip of the flame.
- Although concentration is quite important, it is not absolutely essential for full divination benefits to be achieved. (For using this exercise to calm and focus the mind, see p. 66.)
- Try to synchronise your breathing with the movement of the flame and make an effort to control both your breathing and the flame.
- As before, resist the temptation to blink for as long as possible. When tears begin to form in your eyes, very slowly close them and cover them with the palms of your hands. Within moments the after-image of the flame will appear.
- Hold the image in your mind for as long as possible, and when it begins to fade and becomes fragmented, open your eyes, return your gaze to the flame and repeat the whole process.
- Ideally, the exercise should be repeated at least three times in succession. Candle gazing will encourage activity in the creative areas of the brain, a prerequisite for the cultivation of clairvoyance. It is always a good idea to integrate it into your training programme.

The after-image effect will help to familiarise you with the inner world of form and colour, and will allow you to have some understanding of complementary or astral colours. In Buddhism the after-image effect of scrying is termed the *Kasina* and is an integral part of meditation.

Palmistry

God sealeth the hand of every man, that all men may know his work.

JOB 37:7

This quote comes from the Old Testament, but there are even more ancient references to palmistry in Vedic texts from India dating back 3,000 years. The ancients of the East regarded the art of reading hands as a precise science, and although the majority of their practices have been lost over time, some of them were handed down and became an integral part of Romany tradition.

The Western world first became interested in palmistry through the writings of Aristotle. Aristotle gained his knowledge of palm-reading from ancient Egyptian texts discovered on an altar dedicated to Thoth, the god of writing and wisdom. Other Greek philosophers also expressed a strong belief in the power of palm-reading.

Today palm-reading, or chiromancy to use its correct name, can be seen at any fairground or seaside resort. There are people who regard themselves as serious 'palm analysts' rather than palmists.

While some readers merely use the hand as a focal point and glean their information from their psychic skills, the expert considers the lines on the palm and their patterns, as well as the shape and size of the hand and the individual fingers. Recently, one of the guests on my television programme *Secrets* was author and hand analyst Tre McCamley, one of the most proficient I have ever had the pleasure of consulting. Although she knew very little about me, her analysis based on a reading of my hands was uncannily accurate. She told me every detail of my life, from my early days as a musician living and travelling in Europe to my health problems and career. I must admit I was truly amazed! Her book, *Palm Decoder*, is one of the most informative on the subject and well worth reading.

There is no doubt that there is much more to palmistry than most people imagine, and as a method of divination it is certainly one of the most accurate. There is an association with astrology, as various parts of the hand are named after different planets. The subject is complex, and I recommend that you read as much as you can about it. You might even like to think about attending a seminar or signing up for a course.

The Tarot

Tarot cards are one of the most popular methods of divination. Their exact origins are unknown, but it is believed that the system started in Italy during the Renaissance. Although the Tarot is now used as a tool of prophecy, its symbols have a much deeper spiritual meaning and represent an ancient core of secret wisdom.

The pack consists of two parts: the 22 trump cards, known as the *Major Arcana* (arcana means secrets), and the four suits, collectively called the *Minor Arcana*. Traditionally, the Major Arcana depicted scenes and people and the Minor Arcana usually showed the appropriate number of symbols from the particular suit – the Ten of Cups showing ten cups forming a pattern, the Two of Swords depicting two crossed swords, and so on. However, over the years this tradition has been modified and today many different Tarot sets are available.

Although most clairvoyants only use Tarot cards as a focal point for their psychic skills, many serious readers have made a study of the symbolism of the cards and use this as a means of interpreting the future. Another approach is simply to relate the pictures to situations and events in a person's life and rely on intuition to give guidance.

I once knew a clairvoyant called Mavis who had been blind from birth, although this did not stop her giving readings with Tarot cards. After a client had carefully selected their cards, Mavis would spread them across the table, focus on them for a few moments, then very slowly move her hands over them, without touching them, before she began to interpret the feelings that came intuitively to her. I must say her readings were deadly accurate and the predictions she made always came true. When I asked how she managed this, she told me she simply felt the energy from the individual cards themselves. She knew her cards so well that when she was working with them she was somehow able to have a deep spiritual relationship with them.

The Runes

The runes are a method of divination consisting of small tablets of either wood or stone inscribed with runic symbols. It is not certain where exactly runes originated, although runic inscriptions have been discovered dating from as far back as AD 3. They are regarded as a sacred writing system. The word 'rune', which can be found in various forms in both Germanic and Celtic languages, literally means 'a mystery' or 'holy secret' that is 'whispered'. Germanic tribes of northern Europe passed the runic tradition on to Britain, Scandinavia, Iceland and other parts of the world, and there is some evidence to suggest that it was still used in some parts of the world up until the seventeenth century, as runic inscriptions have been discovered on graves, buildings, weapons and even tools. It is interesting that early Christians branded anyone found in possession of runic staves a heretic and burned them to death, as the runes were looked upon as an affront to God.

In ancient times wise men and women used the runes when seeking to resolve many of their tribal problems, and held that they possessed sacred powers capable of setting them free spiritually and opening their consciousness to God-like influences. The spiritual implications of the runes suggest that they can help us to achieve wholeness and harmony, and also to create that bridge of consciousness between ourselves and the higher spiritual worlds. Strictly speaking, the runes should not really be used for fortune-telling, but rather to offer us a greater insight into our deeper, more spiritual natures.

As with all such spiritual systems of divination, there are both simple and complex methods of reading the runes. Should the runic system of divination hold a special attraction for you, then read as much as you can about it and leave no runic stone unturned.

Astrology

Astrology has been used as a system of divination for millennia. Although its origins are not clear, it is believed to have been developed in ancient Mesopotamia as early as 2000 BC. Today even the sceptic cannot resist the temptation to take a sly peek at the astrological column in the daily newspaper to see how their day is going to go.

Most people appreciate, however, that what is written in the daily tabloids is only a general look at each of the 12 astrological signs, and that in order for a more specific personal forecast to be given the exact time and location of birth are required. From these details an experienced astrologer is able to create an accurate 'natal chart', which gives enough information about a person for a detailed analysis of their life to be made.

Some years ago an elderly lady drew up my astrological chart, and although she knew nothing whatsoever about me the chart illustrated the most difficult years of my life and even highlighted the exact time when I would emerge from the mire. It was uncannily accurate.

An experienced astrologer can also create a chart to answer specific questions, such as 'Where did I lose my wedding ring?' This is called a 'horary chart'.

In fact astrological charts can be created for almost anything. An 'event chart' is able to predict the eruption of a volcano or determine the time, or outcome, of a major event. It is believed the Magi, the three wise men in the traditional story of the birth of Jesus, belonged to a select priestly order which prophesied the birth through astrological calculations at least 100 years before it actually took place.

The most beneficial time to initiate a major business change or begin a new enterprise can also be determined through a carefully calculated astrological chart. Adolf Hitler and Napoleon Bonaparte, two of the most infamous dictators the world has known, always consulted their personal astrologers before embarking upon an important campaign. Julius Caesar, too, frequently drew up his battle plans in consultation with his astrologer.

Although strictly speaking I am not an astrologer, I do practise something I call 'intuitive astrology'. This involves a person's date of birth, their outward appearance and my intuitive assessment of them. I do this purely as a form of entertainment at the beginning of some of my shows. Although a traditional astrologer would most probably decry my method of working, it is effective and can be very accurate. I use it purely as a way of divining a person's future, and always emphasise that it is in no way related to any traditional system of the very ancient science of astrology. In saying this, though, I should point out that you will need some knowledge of the astrological signs. You can easily find out more by reading any of the hundreds of books on astrological interpretation.

Dowsing

Of all divinatory tools, dowsing is perhaps the only one that is taken really seriously by the general public, primarily because dowsers have been used successfully in the oil industry to find new sources and also by the police to locate missing persons. Hazel twigs were traditionally used to dowse for water, and in America dowsing rods are still used today in a drought to locate underground water sources.

Using a pendulum

The most popular method of dowsing is with a pendulum, such as a crystal or a weight of some kind on a length of string. This is usually held over an object or objects until it moves in some way, indicating 'yes' or 'no' in reply to the dowser's question.

Getting to know your pendulum

- ◆ Before using a pendulum you must first of all become accustomed to its vibrations by sitting quietly with it in your hands. You must create the feeling that the pendulum is a visible extension of your mind, and that it will visibly convey the appropriate information to you.

- ◆ Next, you must establish which is the 'yes' and which is the 'no' by holding the string and allowing the pendulum to hang loosely over the palm of your other outstretched hand.

- ◆ Ask a simple question, such as 'Am I male?' and make a note of which way the pendulum moves, clockwise or anticlockwise.

- ◆ Then follow this with the question 'Am I female?' The crystal should move the other way.

Once you have established which is the 'yes' and which 'no', the pendulum is ready to be used.

Remember only to ask a question that requires a 'yes' or a 'no' answer and not one that requires the crystal to make a choice, such as 'Am I a male or female?' This is common sense.

You can use your pendulum to locate things you have mislaid. Try the following exercise.

Finding lost objects

◆ Ask a friend to hide a ring or some other small item in a room.

◆ Hold your pendulum loosely and then move slowly around the room, mentally asking, 'Is it here?' Wait for the response from the pendulum.

◆ When you obtain a positive response, you should be able to find what your friend has hidden.

As with all tools of divination, experimentation will produce the best results.

Psychic Handwriting Analysis

It was while I was appearing at a theatre in Southport some years ago that I realised just how much mediums are at the mercy of the spirit world and those who dwell there. For the whole of the first part of the show there was no communication from the spirit world whatsoever, forcing me to work psychically with the audience. This meant I had to do auric readings and use any other psychic means I could to glean information for selected members of the audience. I did not want to repeat this experience, and knew I had to develop something else I could use in the show. Just by chance I discovered that when I touched an example of someone's handwriting images would pass quickly through my mind. Also, when I was holding a sample of handwriting, someone from the spirit world would sometimes communicate with me, and I could strengthen my link with them by means of the writing. This gave me the idea of performing psychic handwriting analysis.

Psychic handwriting analysis is not graphology, but is simply a method of divination in which information is gleaned from a person's handwriting. I must make it clear that I know very little about graphology itself, which requires fairly intensive handwriting analysis. Psychic handwriting analysis is a completely different concept. As we do not have the space to cover this extensive subject here, I can only scratch the surface of how it is done.

Practising psychic handwriting analysis

There is no ABC of learning psychic handwriting analysis. If you have creative tendencies and a reasonably good eye for shape, texture and colour, then you will more than likely be able to do it.

◆ Ask a friend to give you a piece of handwriting by someone unknown to you.

◆ Simply glance briefly at the writing. Do not make an attempt to analyse the curves and slopes of the writing, as a graphologist would do, as this will only confuse you.

◆ In this way you will automatically initiate the mental process of psychic analysis. Images, feeling, shapes, objects and even names will eventually come into your mind.

◆ You can check your accuracy by asking for feedback from your friend.

Psychic handwriting analysis is one of those psychic processes that either works for you or doesn't. You will either have a feeling for it or you won't – it is as simple as that! However, to repeat the familiar mantra, practice does make perfect.

Now it's time to take a look at healing and self-healing, the ninth step in your programme.

Healing and Self-healing

It never ceases to amaze me how a bright sunny day can make us feel uplifted when we are under the weather and how those grey and gloomy days make us feel depressed. The cliché 'It's all in the mind' carries more truth than we realise, for sometimes the way we feel is solely dependent upon the weather, the people with whom we associate and the environment in which we live. In fact, our minds are continually being bombarded by outside influences – even the decor of our home can influence our mood.

If we could only realise the true potential of our minds, disease would probably be a thing of the past. Nothing would be beyond the bounds of possibility. For most people all this is pure science fiction. The fact is, though, that we are all capable of greater things, and by using the power of our minds we can not only influence other people but also fashion a brighter and healthier future for ourselves.

The growing interest in the complementary approach to medicine today has also given rise to an increased interest in spiritual healing and related methods. These are far from new. All ages and civilisations have practised some form of energy transference to heal the sick. Yogi masters have been practising healing for over 26 centuries.

In the West, the early Church exploited healing and promoted the belief that it was a 'special' gift possessed by 'certain kinds' of people. This was simply a form of control, as the priests of the early Church had a monopoly on healing and branded as heretics anyone who threatened their power. In fact, everyone possesses the ability to heal to a greater or lesser degree, and this ability is not in any way dependent upon religious persuasion or belief in any particular god.

Breath, Heat and Movement

Ancient Greek physicians administered healing through the laying on of hands and limb manipulation. Their leading practitioner, Asclepius, carefully breathed on the diseased parts of the body then applied a gentle rubbing motion with his hands. The ancient Druids also conducted their healing ceremonies in this way, and historical records show that Druid priests were able to cure a range of illnesses.

Wise physicians, even among the ancients, have always been aware of how beneficial it is to the blood to make gentle hand movements over the body. This method has been found to be effective with sudden as well as habitual pains, and in various forms of debility, being both renovating and strengthening. Today many experienced doctors believe that the heat of the hand is highly beneficial to the sick.

Magnetic Healing

Magnetism is active everywhere, and there is nothing new in it but the name; it is a paradox only to those who ridicule everything, and who attribute to the power of Satan whatever they are unable to explain.

VAN HELMONT

In the seventeenth century, when the chemist and physician Van Helmont was writing, a Scotsman by the name of Maxwell was practising and teaching the art of magnetic healing. Although this was looked upon with some disdain by the Church, Maxwell's belief in a vital spirit that pervaded everything and could be tapped into to heal the sick caught the imagination of his numerous devotees.

A similar idea surfaced in 1734, when a priest by the name of Father Hehl propagated the idea of a 'Universal Fluid' that could be used to cure all manner of illnesses. Needless to say Father Hehl was branded a heretic and driven from the Church.

At the end of the eighteenth century, Friedrich Anton Mesmer, the innovator of mesmerism, the forerunner to hypnotism, taught the radical and unconventional theory of animal magnetism. Initially, he was held in high esteem in Vienna and Paris, and was looked upon as a sort of a guru of his day. The Prussian government established a hospital devoted to the application of magnetic healing, and such was the interest in the subject that strict laws were passed by various Continental governments to prevent anyone outside the medical profession from using magnetic treatments. Nonetheless, Mesmer and his ideas fell into disfavour, and some of his followers seized the opportunity to exploit the knowledge they had obtained from him, thus prostituting what they had learned. However, their interpretation of his teachings did give birth to new schools of thought.

Magnetic Healing versus Spiritual Healing

Magnetic healing has often been confused with spiritual healing. This misconception is still harboured today by a lot of people who actually practise magnetic healing in the belief that they are administering spiritual healing.

Magnetic, or pranic, healing involves the transmission of a person's own energies, and while there are different theories as to how this process takes place, it is an ability we all possess to a greater or lesser degree. Spiritual healing involves a certain degree of attunement with the patient, and also a blending of the healer's mind with a higher power.

In my experience, spiritual healing necessitates some degree of spiritual attainment and discipline but very little technique, while the effectiveness of magnetic or pranic healing is primarily dependent upon ability and technique.

Although pranic healing is best administered by a healthy person, someone who is unwell can facilitate the movement of prana in their own body in the following way.

Pranic healing exercise

◆ Sit comfortably on a straight-backed chair, close your eyes and breathe rhythmically for a few minutes until your mind is still and you feel quite relaxed.

◆ Press the palms of your hands together in the praying position in front of you, and as you slowly inhale move your hands apart.

◆ As you exhale, bring them together again.

◆ Continue doing this, and imagine intense white light passing from one palm to the other. Each time you press your hands together, imagine the power of the energy increasing. Your imagination will encourage the movement of energy in your hands, and the longer the exercise continues the more intense the force will feel as it passes from one hand to the other.

◆ Continue this process for around seven minutes. By now your hands should feel quite warm and be tingling with energy.

◆ Finally, place one hand on either side of your head while continuing to breathe rhythmically.

Visualisation should be an integral part of this exercise – the more you are able to visualise the force as intense white light, the more power will emanate from your hands.

Once you have mastered this method of generating energy, you should be able to pass it on to others for the purpose of calming taut nerves, easing pain and taking away fear and anxiety. This healing method is also effective in the process of soothing inflammation, and will coagulate the flow of blood from a flesh wound. However, it must be said that, unlike spiritual healing, pranic healing can only be applied as a temporary form of treatment, an emergency measure, as generally speaking the results do not last.

Remember also that, where healing is concerned, motive is far more important than action, for it is the motive which ultimately produces the results. And the old adage 'Physician, heal thyself!' remains important. All too many practitioners administer healing when they themselves are quite unwell. And so before we take a look at the various healing methods, we must first of all explore self-healing.

Self-healing

While the mind has the power to heal, it equally has the power to destroy. A worried, stressed or anxious person is usually someone who has no control over their mental processes. Eventually the mind short-circuits, causing the body to break down and allowing illness to develop. Everyone is subject to stress at some time in their life, of course, and everyone deals with it in different ways. Some people find it difficult to cope and crumple under the strain. Others thrive on the adrenalin rush and use the energy to deal with their day-to-day situations.

In order to cope well with stress, your mind needs to be controlled and focused. The only way this can be easily and successfully achieved is through meditation. We have already looked at ways in which you can incorporate meditation into your 10-step programme (see Step 4), but once you have mastered whichever technique you have chosen to use, you might like to try the following healing meditations.

Power meditation

◆ Sit on a straight-backed chair, making sure that your chest, neck and head are as nearly in a straight line as possible, with your shoulders thrown slightly back and your hands resting lightly on your lap.

◆ Make your mind still by breathing rhythmically for a few moments.

◆ With your eyes closed, picture on the screen of your mind a lake – a very placid lake – with, behind it, hills silhouetted against a clear blue sky. Project yourself into the picture, imagine yourself standing on the grassy bank of the lake, and experience it all as though you are actually there.

◆ See the sun very bright in the sky, shining on the surface of the lake. Feel the sunshine on your skin and the gentle breeze ruffling your hair. Hear the rustling leaves on the trees behind you.

◆ Try to feel at one with this beautiful scene and be overwhelmed by a sense of peace.

◆ As you gaze out across the lake, feel the rays of the sun passing through you like some powerful healing force.

◆ Feel the blue of the sky moving slowly down to surround you. Sense it moving around your body, soothing and healing your nerves, muscles, cells, tissue and fibres, rejuvenating your whole being.

◆ No matter what is wrong with you, feel the golden light of the sun and the blue of the sky restoring your vitality and making you well.

◆ Remain on the bank of the lake, overwhelmed by the golden and blue rays, for as long as you feel comfortable, then, to conclude the meditation, simply allow the picture to fade from your mind, and relax.

◆ Finish off with some slow rhythmic breathing, as this helps close down the screen of the mind.

Invasion therapy

For a more specific form of meditative healing, a more mentally interactive approach is needed. Anything can be treated through the following method of mental 'invasion therapy', but results are dependent on the extent of your belief in the method and your ability to make it work.

◆ Either relax in a comfortable chair or lie on your bed, whichever you prefer.

◆ Begin as before with some slow rhythmic breathing.

◆ Focus your mind on the diseased part of the body and allow your attention to remain there for at least five minutes or so.

◆ Breathe deeply, feeling as though you are drawing the breath in through that particular part of your anatomy, and with each exhalation see yourself infusing it with energy and vitality.

◆ Repeat this process over and over until you tire of it.

◆ Still mentally focusing upon the diseased part of your body, try to picture it as being extremely dark in colour, in comparison with the rest of your body, which is intense white light.

◆ Spend some time focusing on the dark, diseased part of your body and, still breathing rhythmically, gradually feel intense white light streaming into the affected area. Let there be plenty of movement as it infuses the dark area of your body and transforms it into white light.

◆ Repeat this process over and over until you are quite satisfied that your entire body is radiating intense white light.

◆ Close the meditation down by once again breathing rhythmically, then slowly allow the picture to fade from your mind, and relax.

The healing process is influenced by the mental interaction with the physical anatomy, which can have quite a powerful effect not just on the diseased part but on your body as a whole. In fact the holistic effects of this technique can produce some dramatic results. The meditation can also be used to revitalise you when you are feeling tired or under the weather.

Breathing

Most Eastern traditions teach that there is a universal energy that helps to maintain the health and balance of the body, and that when this energy ceases to be present, death occurs. This life force is to be found in the food we eat, in the water we drink, and primarily in the air we breathe, hence the saying 'Breath is life'.

Shallow breathing is in fact one of the main causes of poor health – not just physically, but also in terms of emotional and psychological health. When you are stressed your breathing becomes shallow and quick, your heartbeat quickens and you perspire. We have all experienced these symptoms of anxiety and stress at some time or another in our lives – they are the body's way of coping with a threatening situation. Should you allow this state of heightened alertness to persist over a period of years, however, your health will suffer in some way as a consequence.

Of course, coping with stress is easier said than done. It clouds the judgement and distorts the perception. It can make you irritable and irrational. A person who lives constantly under the threat of anxiety is usually a person who has become sensitised to feeling. The way to freedom is to desensitise the body and the mind. Breathing correctly is of paramount importance here, as this not only quietens the mind but also slows down the heart and calms the nerves. You might like to try the following exercise.

Breathing exercise

◆ Sit on a straight-backed chair as comfortably as possible, with your spine fairly straight.

◆ Breathe in and out for a few minutes, expanding your diaphragm as you breathe in and drawing it in as you breathe out.

◆ With your eyes closed, draw the breath in through your nostrils and see it passing down the airways into your lungs.

◆ Hold the breath for a few seconds, and in your mind's eye see it circulating in your solar plexus. In yoga the solar plexus is known as the 'sun centre', and it is here that prana is stored.

◆ As you exhale, blow the air forcibly out through pursed lips, emptying your lungs completely.

◆ Repeat the process for at least ten minutes. (A word of warning, though: try not to make it a labour, as this only defeats the object of the exercise.)

◆ When you feel nice and relaxed, still with your eyes closed, place your fingertips gently on your solar plexus.

◆ Breathe in slowly, and as you do so see the incoming breath in your mind's eye as pure energy or white light. Watch it moving down into your solar plexus in great streams.

◆ Hold the breath while carrying the white light in your fingertips to your head. Place your fingertips gently on your forehead, and breathe the white light through your fingertips into your head. In your mind, see your head being flooded with white light.

◆ When your breath has been fully expelled, once again hold it, then return your fingertips to your solar plexus and repeat the process.

This exercise can bring about remarkable physiological and psychological changes. It is known to relieve stress and headaches caused by tension, and is an ideal way of revitalising the nervous system, particularly when you are feeling under the weather. To the cynic I would say try it before you criticise this technique. You may be surprised.

The next exercise is a very effective way of instigating balance, and can also be used to ease pain.

Creating balance in the body

- ◆ Relax in a comfortable chair.

- ◆ Imagine that your body is infested with black killer ants. In your mind's eye see the ants crawling around inside your body, especially in any area where you are experiencing disease or pain.

- ◆ Breathe rhythmically for a few moments to make your mind still, then in your mind's eye create a large white beetle. See this creature moving around inside your body, radiating intense white light, which passes through you rather like electricity.

- ◆ As the beetle moves slowly through you, watch it devouring the black ants.

- ◆ Make quite certain that all the ants have been devoured before you conclude the exercise.

- ◆ As always, end your visualisation with some slow rhythmic breathing.

- ◆ Practise this every day for at least 10 to 15 minutes.

(Should you find insects repulsive, then substitute the invasion therapy exercise – see p. 165.)

To reiterate something I said earlier, do not underestimate the importance of this exercise because of its simplicity. The mind is extremely powerful and the body is at its mercy. Lack of faith in the technique merely creates barriers preventing the healing process from taking place.

Spiritual Healing

Once you have worked on healing yourself, you can turn your attention to healing others. First of all, try the following quiz.

So you want to be a healer?

1. Do your hands ever feel extremely warm, or perhaps tingle when you are close to someone who is unwell?
2. Do you feel overwhelmed by compassion when you see a disabled or an elderly person struggling to get around?
3. Do you sometimes find a friend or neighbour who is unwell constantly coming into your thoughts?
4. Do people always say they feel better after spending a short time with you?
5. Do some people drain you of energy after only a short time in their company?
6. Do you seem to have a lot of static electricity in your body, causing you to get a shock from certain things and people you touch?

If you answered 'yes' to all these, the chances are you possess the potential to be a healer. Now answer these questions.

1. Do you bathe every day?
2. Do you smoke?
3. Is your intake of alcohol excessive?

4. Are you a vegetarian, and if not are you nonetheless conscious of what you eat?

5. Are you sensitive to personal odours?

6. Are you affected by fluorescent lighting?

7. Do you change your underwear and socks every day?

Generally speaking 2 and 3 are the only questions to which the answer should be 'no'. However, although it would be preferable for a healer not to smoke or drink to excess, neither of these vices would prevent you from becoming one. It may sound ridiculous, but changing socks and underwear before administering healing is not important only for hygiene reasons, but also can have a psychological effect on you.

Basic Guidelines for Healing

The correct approach

During the process of administering healing it is important to eliminate self-consciousness. This is probably easier said than done, at least until you develop confidence in yourself and what you are able to achieve. But until you are able to focus your consciousness directly on to your patient you will more than likely impose limitations upon your healing ability and the process as a whole.

Once you have your first patient in front of you there will be no time for you to change your mind about giving the session. Your patient will be seeking your reassurance as well as your healing. You need therefore to apply yourself to the healing process with enough confidence to encourage the patient to relax and have faith in your ability.

The correct approach is important. Although most healers choose to be silent during the healing process, in the early stages it is a good idea to talk to your patient occasionally. As well as offering them reassurance, this puts them at ease and makes them feel more comfortable.

I am quite certain that after your first six healing treatments you will see a remarkable transformation in your confidence. I'll say it again – practice makes perfect, and the more you work as a healer the more proficient you will become.

A code of practice

No matter what method of healing you use, there is a very important code of practice that you should always follow.

A healer is always advised never to administer treatment alone to a member of the opposite sex. (In fact it is always a good idea to have someone else in attendance, unless of course you know the patient extremely well.)

Certainly a male healer should never apply healing directly to any private part of a woman's anatomy. It is not necessary for a patient to remove any items of clothing in order to receive the full effect of the healing treatment. Healing works at a subtle level and is able to penetrate any garments, regardless of how many the patient is wearing. Some healers treat only the head and shoulders, and still produce remarkable results on other parts of the body.

Unless you are actually qualified in the art of body manipulation, it is unwise either to apply any pressure to painful limbs or to move them in an attempt to make them more supple. This sort of treatment has nothing whatsoever to do with spiritual healing. Although you may feel it looks impressive, it may cause further discomfort, or even permanent damage. This form of treatment should be left to the expertise of a physiotherapist.

Remember that a spiritual healer is nearly always consulted as a last resort. It is important therefore that you do not offer the patient false hope. Try to be as positive as you possibly can without making any wild statements or promises you may not be able to fulfil.

It is also important to avoid any outlandish or totally uncon-ventional methods that may only serve to make the patient uneasy. Be as natural and as friendly as possible, even if it means designing a completely different treatment and dialogue for each patient.

Remember these vital points:

◆ Do not offer a diagnosis.

◆ Do not offer advice regarding medication.

◆ Do not tell the patient to stop taking medication.

◆ Do not administer healing to a member of the opposite sex by yourself.

◆ Do not apply healing to any private part of a person's anatomy.

◆ Do not request that clothing be removed.

◆ Unless trained to do so, never manipulate a painful limb.

◆ Do not make any psychic assessments either of a person's life or their health.

Healing sessions should be limited to no more than two hours initially, at least until you become more proficient and accustomed to dealing with different people. Although you may apportion this time equally between your patients, you may find that extra time is required by one of the more serious cases. Remember always to be disciplined, and do not permit anyone to take up your time and energy unnecessarily, as this will only result in the deterioration of your own health.

Because some people perspire during the healing treatment, it is always a good idea to observe basic rules of hygiene by washing your hands after each treatment. This process will also have a psychological effect, making it easier to separate one patient from the next.

Some healers make use of a treatment bed when working. Rather than putting a person at ease, however, this may make them feel vulnerable. Until a person is accustomed to the way you work, it may be better to allow them to sit on a chair with a straight back or, even better, a stool, to enable you to access their back easily. However, a treatment bed does have its advantages. Having the patient lying in front of you means that the entire body can be accessed without any great effort, particularly when applying treatment to the spine.

Healing by instinct

Although most healers have their own particular methods, unless you possess a reliable psychic ability it is always best to allow your instincts to guide your hands. In fact, the more you employ your intuitive skills, the more reliable they will become.

Some healers claim to 'see' health problems psychically, while others claim to 'see' or 'feel' nothing at all. Psychic abilities can have a powerful effect in spiritual healing, helping to bring about recovery or simply easing discomfort or pain. During the healing treatment, take every opportunity to exercise your psychic skills. Whatever your psychic abilities, it does help the healing process if you seek to mentally 'drive out' the disease.

Regardless of what methods you employ, the responsibility involved in what you are doing must always be borne in mind. The person to whom the healing is being administered will most probably be relying totally upon you. Remember that you are not medically trained, so are not qualified to offer advice about a person's health.

In the initial stages it is very easy to become obsessed with the actual practice of healing. Avoid, at all costs, becoming over-enthusiastic, as this will only deplete your own energy levels and will probably make the healing less effective. Common sense must always prevail if your are to become a good and well-respected healer.

Attuning to your patient

Some healers begin the healing process by sitting in front of the patient and holding their hands, while others prefer to begin by standing behind the seated patient with a hand on each of their shoulders. There are no set rules – it is all a matter of personal preference. The initial procedure is purely a process of attunement to help you focus your mind on the patient.

Once your mind is attuned to the mind of the patient it will become easier for you to access their personal energies, thus enabling the healing to take place.

Deciding when to conclude the period of attunement is again a matter of judgement rather than any hard and fast rules. You must be guided by your instincts through the entire treatment.

Beginning the treatment

Once attunement with your patient has well and truly been established it is nearly always a good idea to begin the healing treatment with the head. Bear in mind, though, that some people do not like their head to be touched, so until you get to know your patient it might be a good idea to begin by holding your hands to either side of their head, an inch or so away.

Allow your hands to remain in this position until a little heat has been created. Be guided instinctively as to the appropriate length of time, and then slowly move your hands to the shoulders, placing one on each.

Although it will not take you very long to discover your own method of working, I always find it extremely effective to slowly work down the spine, mentally moving the energy during the entire process. It is quite surprising how much comfort is derived when healing is applied to the spine, beginning at the base of the skull and slowly working down towards the lower part of the back.

By placing one hand on the back, around the lung area, and the other hand on the corresponding part of the chest at the front, it is possible to cause the energy to move through the respiratory system, thus enabling the patient to derive more benefit from the healing. This treatment has a remarkable effect, especially if the patient's breathing is laboured as a result of a problem with the lungs. It also encourages the whole body to relax by moving the energy more effectively through the blood, nerves and muscles.

Spinal healing treatment

This healing treatment moves energy round the whole body and has an anaesthetising effect upon any inflammatory or painful conditions. It can also be effective in alleviating emotional or psychological conditions, or any stress-related illness.

For this treatment your patient will need to lie face down.

◆ Beginning at the base of the skull, place a hand on the patient's neck and locate the beginning of their spine using your index finger and thumb.

◆ Hold the spine gently between the thumb and forefinger, without applying any pressure, and slowly move them down until the coccyx is reached.

◆ Repeat the process, beginning again at the base of the skull. This time, however, apply a little mental interaction by visualising your thumb and index finger moving energy freely down the spine. It is a good idea to 'see' the energy as pure white light pulsating vibrantly as you trace the course of the spine.

◆ Repeat this process five or six times and then reverse it, beginning this time at the coccyx. Now, however, use the thumb and index finger of one hand to manipulate the energy while following this up with the other hand placed gently across the spine.

Hand rotation treatment

This treatment may be used in conjunction with the previous one. It is an extremely powerful way of encouraging the flow of energy in the body and helping recovery from illness. The technique is invigorating and helps to stimulate the major glands of the body, producing a cleansing effect on the blood and nervous system. It can also be used as a general tonic.

To ensure that the best results are achieved, the patient needs to lie face up.

- ◆ Place one hand over the area of the throat, without touching it, and with your fingers outspread.

- ◆ Hold your other hand over the first, without touching it, the fingers positioned in the same way.

- ◆ Slowly rotate the first hand in a clockwise motion, while simultaneously rotating the second hand in an anticlockwise motion.

- ◆ Allow the circular motion of the hands to continue for a few moments before moving to the next point, approximately over the area of the heart. If possible, it is far better to allow the rotation of the hands to continue while moving them from the throat to the heart.

- ◆ Repeat the same process over the heart, then slowly move to the area just below the ribs on the left-hand side of the body. Keep the rotation consistent.

- ◆ Move on to the area of the navel, lingering here a little longer than at the other points, then slowly move your rotating hands to the lower groin.

- ◆ Spend a little longer still in this area before concluding the treatment by sweeping the whole body with your slowly rotating hands, moving from the groin to the head, backwards and forwards three or four times, before finally resting your hands on the patient's forehead.

This healing process has a tendency to create quite a lot of heat in the body, should this be required – in the case of a low temperature, for example. Equally, it will cool the body down should there be fever present. If the treatment is repeated over the course of a week there should be visible improvement in the patient's condition.

The rotational movement of your hands encourages the movement of energy from the chakras along the nadis. The movement of your hands is extremely subtle, yet produces a remarkable effect upon the aura and the chakras. The whole treatment is soothing, and often has an anaesthetising effect upon the patient.

Final Points

I should remind you once more that the healer is *not* qualified to offer a diagnosis. Not only is it ethically wrong to do so, but it may give rise to legal issues should your diagnosis be incorrect or cause the patient distress. Never make predictions about the person's health or promise that you will make them well. Where a terminal illness is concerned, at worst spiritual healing will take away the fear of dying; at best it will prolong the patient's life or even encourage remission.

Although I have suggested several healing techniques, everyone has their own unique way of working. Once you feel confident about your healing ability you will probably develop your own method fairly quickly.

In the final step we'll look at how you can protect yourself and those you love against unwanted psychic phenomena throughout your development programme.

Psychic Self-defence

Whatever area of the psychic field you work in, a healthy and well-balanced approach is of great importance. There is no place whatsoever for fanciful notions such the belief that as long as your intentions are good and honourable you will automatically be afforded divine protection and no harm will come to you.

It is true that we are looked after and guided to some extent by angelic forces, but it must also be understood that they are only as strong as *our* weakest point. Also, they may deliberately guide us into difficult situations in order for us to gain greater knowledge and experience.

The best approach is always to work on the premise that a psychic attack will take place at some time and formulate a protective programme as soon as you decide to embark on an exploration of the process of psychic development.

Let's look at how it all works.

Thought Dynamics

Thoughts crystallise into habit, and habits solidify into circumstance.

JAMES ALLEN

To all intents and purposes, we are continually occupying our own private portion of space by virtue of the way we think. Our thoughts are attracted by thoughts of a similar nature and form thought strata in psychic space, in very much the same way that clouds form groups in the atmosphere. However, these thought clouds have different vibratory characteristics, and so the same portion of space may be occupied by a thousand different kinds.

In fact, districts, towns, cities and even nations are permeated by the thoughts of all those who live there and have lived there in the past, and these infiltrate the minds of everyone who comes within range. We are being influenced by the thoughts and feelings of those long gone from this world just as much as by those of the living. Evil released into the psychic atmosphere hundreds and even thousands of years ago is still able to have a powerful effect upon the world today. Perpetrators of past evil are still very much alive, if only by virtue of the force they created when they actually walked the earth.

Although to many this idea will most probably appear far-fetched and fanciful, it is one that has been taught in esoteric circles for thousands of years. The concept of 'thought dynamics' forms an integral part of the philosophical teachings handed down through the ages. A practical aspect of these teachings resides in the strict guidelines that have evolved about psychic infiltration and self-protection when under psychic attack.

The Influence of the Astral World

As well as influencing our physical world, both good and bad thoughts are drawn towards the vibratory structure of the astral world, where they fuel the powers of those discarnate entities that dwell upon the inner astral planes.

The astral world is not a place. It exists within sequences of vibrations, the slowest of which orbit within and around the physical atom. It is in the lowest dimensions of this world that the more rudimentary forms of life exist. Their sole motivation is gratification of their base passions and desires. They are often referred to as 'astral vagabonds', for they roam freely. Although they no longer inhabit a physical body through which to seek their gratification, they delight in feeding off the minds of those who are alive in the physical world. This can be one of the forms of psychic attack.

Psychic Attack

I often think that the term 'psychic attack' is something of a misnomer, as quite often the physical effects are extremely powerful and feel anything but 'psychic'. In fact psychic attack is an umbrella term covering three different phenomena:

1. The discarded mental dross referred to as 'psychic germs'. This can also be an accumulation of thought mass.

2. Psychic attack from a living person with a great deal of psychic power, initiated either consciously or unconsciously.

3. Psychic attack from a discarnate soul, usually one that is malevolent.

We will look at each of these in more detail later.

Although everyone is at risk from psychic attack, the most vulnerable are those endeavouring to develop their psychic skills and those already using their abilities. As mentioned earlier, should you have any history of nervousness, anxiety or other psychological illness it would be wise not to become too involved in the process of psychic development, at least until you have fully recovered. Even then you should tread with some caution and should always be supervised, as you will be more prone to psychic attack and need to exercise extra caution.

Even the experienced psychic occasionally encounters psychic attack of one kind or another, and although they may not be affected in the same way as an inexperienced person, it can still be quite unpleasant. Sickness and headaches are quite common, and in extreme cases there can be acute depression and total disruption of one's life.

However, in the majority of cases, unless the perpetrator sustains the attack, little harm is done to the person targeted. In any case, if there is nothing in the person's aura that responds sympathetically to the vibrations of the attacker, the invading force rebounds and returns to the attacker with additional force. Undeserved malice or hate will likewise rebound and return to the sender. At this point we should remember the ancient precept 'Curses and blessings come home to roost'.

Although you may be dealing with an extremely powerful force, in a psychic attack the invasion is purely a mental process. So as long as your mind is in control, the attacker will have difficulty infiltrating your personal space. The offending force can, in many cases, be eradicated simply by demanding that it leave you alone. We will look at other methods of psychic defence later on.

Psychic germs

Whether you are involved in the psychic field or not, your aura is frequently being invaded by 'psychic germs' – the discarded mental debris that floats around in psychic space, rather like dust particles in the atmosphere. This kind of force has no consciousness but is simply an accumulation of thought mass created by the malevolent former inhabitants of a building or place. It has never experienced life in a physical form.

The electromagnetic substance of the aura attracts this thought mass and, should you be mentally weak, it will gradually infiltrate your aura, affecting your mental and sometimes your physical health. Although it usually causes no real physical harm, it can lead to psychological damage or illness. However, in extreme cases, if it is allowed to persist and the victim makes no attempt to address the problem, it can cause death.

To eliminate psychic germs completely from the aura, all that is required is a positive mental attitude and a simple psychic cleansing process. The aura-cleansing process given earlier is very effective here (see p. 67), and in the initial stages of your development should be used frequently.

Psychic attack by a living person

Unfortunately there are some people who use their psychic skills maliciously to harm others. Anyone can develop psychic abilities, but how you choose to use them is entirely up to you. You can direct streams of mental energy at another person with the intention of harming or healing them. The process may be the same, but the results are completely different. By the same token you can have an incredible effect upon an innocent person simply by disliking or being jealous of them.

Advanced occult practitioners may even create a thought form, perhaps in the image of a demonic being, and direct it towards a person in order to do them harm. Although mentally creating demons sounds horrifying, it is only in extreme cases that any real harm is sustained.

Should you suspect that someone has psychically targeted you, then remove yourself from their environment as quickly as you can. Stop any association with them, and mentally send out the command that the attack process be reversed. Sit quietly and imagine that the perpetrator is opposite you, and tell them in no uncertain terms that *this must stop!* In a lot of cases this is all that is required to terminate the psychic invasion.

Psychic attack by a discarnate mind

This is perhaps the most insidious form of psychic attack, and certainly the most difficult to diagnose. All three forms of attack have more or less the same effects on a person, but sometimes in the early stages of attack by a discarnate mind the victim exhibits symptoms of paranoia and behaves in a way that is completely out of character. Because the perpetrator has no awareness of time as we know it, the attack is often conducted at any time, night or day, preventing the victim from experiencing a normal sleep pattern. More often than not it is lack of sleep which literally wears the person down.

To safeguard against discarnate psychic attack, the following mental process is quite effective.

- Sit quietly with your eyes closed, and breathe slowly and deeply, ensuring that your inhalations and exhalations are evenly spaced.

- When your mind is quiet, surround yourself with a bright golden light, and in that golden light 'see' a bright blue glow around your head.

- Maintain this for a few minutes, then see the blue glow moving slowly down to your heart.

- Allow it to remain there for a few minutes before moving it to your solar plexus. Once again allow it to remain there for a few minutes.

- Conclude the process with some rhythmic breathing.

Possession

On rare occasions psychic attack can produce symptoms very similar to those of possession. Possession itself can be extremely difficult to diagnose – the archetypal possession depicted in movies or novels is often very misleading. The person who is possessed needs to be carefully assessed in case they are suffering from a psychotic illness.

Very often someone with a psychological problem can be so fascinated by the idea of being possessed that they actually become obsessed with it. Even this is dangerous, as the so-called victim's obsession causes a self-induced hypnotic state, encouraging the release of the subconscious mind's own self-created demons, at which point the person totally loses control. This may sound incredible to anyone who has not had the experience, but believe me, it does happen, and it can damage lives. It requires specialist treatment.

Hauntings

Hauntings can also be quite dramatic, even though they are not always the result of a restless or earthbound spirit. More often than not the apparition is no more than a photographic image imprinted in psychic space, rather like a sound recording on the coated surface of a cassette. When a person dies, these images created by them when they were physically alive can be replayed over and over again, rather like the video of an old movie.

In the late nineteenth century, for example, a wedding carriage collided with a drayman's cart in the Duke Street area of Liverpool. Both the bride and bridegroom died instantly from their injuries, devastating the whole community. Up until the Second World War many people claimed to have witnessed the sad event as the whole scenario was replayed on exactly the same day in June every year. This, and many other supernatural occurrences, ceased completely with the outbreak of war. Most paranormal experts agree that the total discord caused across the planet somehow interrupted the supernatural cycle, dissipating the build-up of energy produced by the tragedy.

Not all so-called 'paranormal replays' are visual, as the etheric substance that captures such activity also records the sounds of past events. A small stretch of parkland beside an ancient church in the Childwall area of Liverpool was allegedly the location of the slaughter of many people in a skirmish with Oliver Cromwell's soldiers during the English Civil War. Locally it is known as 'Bloody Acre'. Although now meticulously landscaped, it is an epicentre of paranormal sounds carried from the past. Stand in the very centre of the grassy parkland, around late afternoon, preferably on a wind-free day, and you will hear a cacophony of angry voices and musket fire, a replay of the events of bygone days.

These sorts of ghostly forms have no consciousness and are very often no more than nebulous images moving in the thin psychic air. I am not suggesting, however, that earthbound spirits are never responsible for hauntings. On the contrary! Earthbound spirits can indeed appear seemingly out of thin air and disappear just as quickly. They are often as solid and substantial as you or I, and are nearly always indistinguishable from a flesh-and-blood person.

Very often it is a love of habit which exerts the most powerful control over a discarnate spirit's life. This is why the old man is often seen sitting in his favourite pub, in the same corner where he always used to sit when he was alive, or why the lady in white is often seen casually strolling through the garden, following the same route she always took in life.

In Woolton Hall, again near the Childwall area of Liverpool, the ghostly figure of a smiling monk has been seen on numerous occasions, happily wending his way through the cellars and sometimes the grounds. Woolton Hall has close connections with the Catholic Church, and was in fact once occupied by both monks and nuns. One of the distinguishing features of the 'happy monk' was the fact that he wore green wellington boots – obviously a monk with a sense of humour! On one occasion, after catching sight of the ghostly monk roaming from room to room, an elderly visitor to Woolton Hall was horrified to glimpse him in her car's rear-view mirror on the way home. She frantically pulled over to the kerb, only to discover that the back seat was completely empty. On this occasion it looks as though the monk was a little more than a paranormal replay, and was indeed probably a genuine spirit manifestation.

Such a genuine manifestation is often able to hold a conversation, and there have been occasions when the intervention of spirits has saved a person's life, which suggests that as well as

185

consciousness they also have feelings. There is definitely far more to this universe than we know, and by developing your psychic skills you can increase your awareness of all things, both seen and unseen, which will then enable you to have a much more profound relationship with the universe itself.

However, when you work in the field of the paranormal you must be prepared for all eventualities. When the doors of the mind have been opened the visitors who call can take any form! So it is always wise to protect yourself and be on your guard. Although over the past ten years great scientific strides have been made in paranormal investigation, I believe that we are no nearer now to understanding the true nature of discarnate spirits and the worlds they inhabit.

Our perceptions are vitally important – very little takes place outside the human mind. For example, if I were to take a friend into an old house that I knew to be haunted, but chose not to divulge this information to him, the chances are that he would neither see nor sense anything out of the ordinary. On the other hand, if I allowed him to be privy to the knowledge that the house was haunted, a spooky scenario would have been created in his mind long before he walked through the door, and he would be more receptive to any paranormal activity.

Very few people would actually be afraid to spend the night in a haunted house, as long as they were accompanied by a few friends. But it is a completely different story when we are faced with the prospect of spending the night in such a place alone. The mind creates its own ghosts and demons, and is very often able to perceive what is not really there. The truth is that it is in our nature to embroider our experiences and to create scenarios that appear more frightening than they really are. I am quite certain that this is the reason why there is a universal fascination for ghost stories. Reading a spooky tale allows the reader to keep a safe distance and to experience the weird happenings at second hand, knowing that at any moment they can be banished simply by closing the book. I suppose this is the great difference between a medium and an ordinary person. A medium has the ability to control their psychic experiences and the ordinary person does not. An integral part of this control is psychic protection.

Protective Measures

From the very beginning of my work as a medium it was instilled into me that protection was far better than cure. Although some of the methods I was taught at first seemed simplistic, I now know from experience that when applied correctly they are extremely effective.

Although prevention is always best, the techniques outlined in this programme are curative as well as preventive. They should not be dismissed because of their simplicity, and should be integrated into your daily programme as a matter of course. There is absolutely no excuse for ignorance. During your development the onus is on you to ensure that you are well protected against the unexpected.

Remember, it is very unhealthy to immerse yourself completely in the paranormal, leaving yourself little or no time for the ordinary, everyday things of life. Cluttering your mind with too many paranormal concepts can make you morbid and introspective. This makes you vulnerable and susceptible to psychic invasion. Remember the old saying, 'All work and no play ...'

Some psychic invasions are so subtle that the victim is unaware of what exactly is happening and may put the effects of the attack down to illness or simply being run down. Headaches, lethargy and depression may be due to fatigue, but they may also be the results of psychic attack, and if ignored may, in time, cause serious mental illness. You may never be 100 per cent sure you are the victim of psychic attack, but should you harbour the slightest suspicion that you are on the receiving end of one, do something about it right away. Continuous psychic attack can eventually wear down your resistance to such a degree that it is extremely detrimental to your health. When you have been continuously subjected to psychic attack, your aura becomes sluggish and fragmented, particularly around your head. By infiltrating your aura, the invading forces gradually break down the energies of your mind, making it possible for the attacker to influence you against your will.

As well as being mentally on your guard when doing psychic work, you should also keep an eye on other aspects of your life. The intention of a psychic attacker may not be to invade your physical body or, for that matter, mind, but rather to bring chaos and disorder to your life. A psychic attack can certainly interfere with, or destroy, relationships and the equilibrium of a person's life. I am speaking from personal experience here. I know only too well just what powerful forces you may be up against when you are subjected to a psychic attack.

I mentioned earlier that some years ago I was invited to speak at a prestigious meeting held at Leeds Town Hall. The event went so well that I was asked to be guest speaker at the Greater World Christian Spiritualists' event in London. I felt honoured, and was very aware of the privilege of speaking at this function. I must say, though, that I was also very naïve, and did not realise that my golden opportunity could attract jealousy, envy and even hate that could manifest itself as a powerful antagonistic force.

My son was still a baby, and we had decided to travel down to London as a family in my five-year-old Ford Escort. Two days before the event, for one reason or another, we changed our minds and decided to travel by train. When we arrived at Liverpool's Lime Street station, travellers to London were being informed that a train had been derailed and that all trains to the capital would be an hour late. This was still all right, as we had timed our journey so that we would have a few hours to spare, perhaps to take in some of the sights. However, the train upon which we were travelling got only as far as Crewe before experiencing engine failure. We spent five hours cooped up in an overcrowded carriage, eventually arriving in London at 6.30 p.m., some hours after the event had finished. I had missed the whole thing.

Although everyone was extremely sympathetic, I was very depressed. It wasn't simply that I had missed the chance of a lifetime to demonstrate my skills, there was something more, but I couldn't quite put my finger on it.

We arrived back home totally exhausted, and the following morning I set off in my car to my mother's house, no more than a mile away. Suddenly there was an almighty bang from beneath the bonnet and the car ground to a halt with smoke billowing from the engine. It seemed that we would not have made it to London however we travelled.

You may think all this was just a matter of coincidence, and in fact that was what everyone thought. But within a very short space of time everything went wrong in my life, and no matter what I did to pull myself out of the proverbial mire, something else came along to push me back in.

For some years I mistakenly thought that it had all been orchestrated by the spirit world to make me do exactly what they wanted me to do. In fact I only recently learned from my helpers in the spirit world that it was an extreme psychic attack resulting from the accumulation of feelings against me. As soon as I was made aware of this I somehow became mentally much stronger, and better able to cope with other negative situations.

Methods of Psychic Self-defence

When working in the psychic field it is always advisable to treat any unexpected feelings of depression or anything going drastically wrong in your life as indications of a possible psychic attack. Always err on the side of caution and be prepared.

Constructive visualisation

If you suspect you are under attack, formulate a working programme of constructive visualisation as soon as possible. The following is a simple but very effective method.

◆ Visualise yourself as surrounded by bright light.

◆ Focus your attention on the light and then gradually change it into a bright blue dome of energy. This has a powerful psychological effect upon you and creates a protective shield.

In order for the exercise to produce positive results, the visualisation has to be consistently maintained and practised regularly every day. Any psychic attack should begin to subside within a week, but even then the cleansing visualisation should be continued for a further month.

Positive protection

No matter what the source of the psychic invasion, you must immediately create some form of positive protection for yourself. Here are some useful ideas that will help you.

◆ Wear or carry a piece of amethyst (preferably unpolished) that you have psychically programmed or charged. This is easily done by washing it in clear water, then leaving it to dry in the sunlight. While sitting quietly, hold the piece of amethyst in your hands and mentally infuse it with your own personal feelings of love. Continue this process for at least ten minutes, then place the amethyst on the television (preferably when it is on) for an evening. Leaving a crystal of any kind on a television magnetises it so it can be used in a more effective way.

◆ Before retiring at night, fill your mind with pleasant vibrations. Listen to gentle music while relaxing in a comfortable chair. Always go to bed feeling pleasantly relaxed and serene.

◆ Eliminate clutter from your house by making a concerted effort to become tidier.

◆ Make every effort to avoid confrontational situations and people who are vexatious.

◆ Avoid worrying about trivialities and do not set yourself impossible tasks.

◆ Pay attention to personal hygiene and make an effort to eliminate negative thinking.

◆ Mentally repeat a protective affirmation, such as the Lord's Prayer, or one you have composed yourself, at least twice a day, time permitting. You can also use a phrase that your mother or someone else used to say to you as a child – anything that stimulates the mind and encourages the imagination.

It is also a good idea to abstain from drinking alcohol, at least until you feel that you have the situation under control. Alcohol and drugs weaken the subtle anatomy, making the aura more suscepti- ble to psychic attack. Those with addictive personalities are prime targets for psychic invasion, as their dependency, no matter how slight, shows a personality weakness which makes them easy prey for those seeking either to destroy or to control via psychic means.

If necessary, you might also consult someone with knowledge of psychic matters. This does not have to be a medium, but can be anyone who has studied the paranormal and who can offer objective, sensible advice.

Attacks during sleep

A psychic attack may not always take place when you are awake. Indeed, most psychic invasions come when you are asleep. In this way the invading forces meet you on their own ground, in the lower mental regions of the astral world, where their malevolence is most powerful. Although in such instances the techniques of protection are more or less the same as when dealing with an attack when you are awake, the approach is slightly different inasmuch as specific thought forms need to be created with a particular mission in mind.

While you sleep, and your physical senses are more or less anaesthetised, your consciousness functions in your astral body, that more refined mental vehicle, and it is through this body's senses that you obtain knowledge and information about the astral world.

Most people do not have any recollection of their sojourn in the astral sleep state, but those who do find that their experiences there mostly filter through into their conscious mind in the form of dreams. However, it would be ridiculous to suppose that all dreams are the symbolic results of our astral experiences. The majority are merely the products of over-indulgence of one kind or another, or even our natural way of dealing with stress and anxiety.

A recurring dream, however, is nearly always the result of an astral experience. It may fit into one of two categories. The first is a 'precognitive dream' – that is, a dream from which prophetic information can be gleaned and which usually comes true in time. In the second kind of dream the dreamer is usually in some dangerous situation, or even being killed. It is quite common for them to see themselves as dead. A dream of this nature is very often the result of some sort of psychic attack, and will certainly continue to recur until something is done about it.

A recurring dream featuring an assault upon the dreamer by some form of demon often means that malevolent forces have been set against them. In order to deal with this unfortunate situation a specific thought form needs to be created and mentally released into astral space each night before you go to sleep. I find it comforting to create thought forms in the image of certain saints with whom I had an affinity when I was a child. Although today I am not particularly religious in a traditional sense, I do hold on to the images of these saintly figures, and still feel very safe in their care. In fact, there is nothing whatsoever wrong in using archetypal religious images to protect you when you feel threatened by some unseen predator, as faith can not only move mountains, but can also eradicate evil or maliciousness directed against you.

I experienced a significant psychic attack featuring a recurring dream in 1986, three months after the death of my mother. This time I had no doubt that I was under psychic attack and that the perpetrators were resident in the astral world and had somehow discovered a way into my mind. The attack occurred because my resistance was low and I was in a state of grief. You are always at your most vulnerable when you are at a low ebb or out of sorts.

Apart from my feeling overwhelmed with grief, my general health was not good at this time. I was recovering from a severe chest infection and was coming to the end of a two-week course of very strong antibiotics. My immunity was quite low and I was feeling very weak.

The attack began with a strange and yet extremely real dream that eventually turned into a nightmare. In the dream I was living in a large Victorian house. It was the middle of the night and I was making my way from my bedroom to the bathroom on the other side of a long corridor. As I glanced down the corridor, the door of the room at the far end was open. Although I was alone in the house I was shocked to see a very stout elderly lady in a black nightdress sitting on a bed smiling at me. She rose from the bed and called out, 'Hello, Mr Roberts ...' I could see she was coming towards me so I said politely, 'Hello, how are you?' Her smile quickly changed to a look of anger. 'You don't even know me,' she snarled. 'You're not interested in my well-being.' She ran towards me and I moved quickly into the bathroom and fumbled nervously to put the catch on the door.

At that point I woke up, sweating profusely, my heart pounding hard against my ribs. The nightmare hung over me for the rest of the day, and although I tried to reassure myself that it was no more than a bad dream, I was dreading the night to come.

As I feared, the dream recurred that night and every night for the next six months. Each night events progressed a little farther. The final straw came when the woman stabbed me in the side with a knife with a long black blade and I woke up in a panic.

Later that day I developed a strange mark on my side, rather like a scar from an old wound. This remained there long enough for me to show an old friend, an experienced occultist. He told me this was a classic example of psychic attack, and gave me stern warnings about worse things to come if I did not defend myself. Fortunately he also told me how to eliminate the dream and prevent further dreams from occurring. It was quite a simple process, but it worked, and as a result I was able to free myself of the dream.

Psychic self-defence in sleep

- First of all, don't be afraid to go to bed. Fear weakens your resistance and gives more power to your attacker.
- Before going to sleep, lie quietly for a while, going over the events of the dream in your mind.
- Create a strategy and prepare yourself to approach your dream intruder as you would an intruder in your home. They are an uninvited guest. The mistake I made was to ask the woman how she was, instead of asking angrily *who* she was.
- When you are satisfied that you are sufficiently prepared, allow yourself to fall asleep.
- In the dream you must walk boldly towards the intruder and demand that they leave your home.
- Even if you are attacked, hold your ground. Showing fear of the attack makes it real and empowers the perpetrator. *It is*

a dream and no more. And although you are doing the dreaming, the dream was created by someone else. Once you have accepted this fact, the dream will cease to be a threat and will dissolve, never to be repeated. This is as true of any threatening situation as it is of a dream.

There are other ways of protecting yourself in your sleep. Here are a couple you might like to try out.

Centring the consciousness

◆ Each night before going to sleep, lie quietly on your bed with your eyes fixed on a certain spot on the ceiling.

◆ Begin to breathe rhythmically – slowly, deeply and evenly.

◆ Resist the temptation to blink for as long as possible, but when your eyes move out of focus, slowly close them and see the after-image of the room.

◆ Let a sense of peace overwhelm you.

◆ In your mind create a beautiful pool of pulsating blue light, the blue of a clear sky on a summer's day. Let this pool of blue light be full of movement, almost alive. See it very clearly in your mind. Imagine it surrounding you and almost filling your bedroom.

◆ Across the surface of this pool create a golden equal-armed cross, whose intersecting lines establish four points of contact at the circumference of the pool of blue light. In this way your sacred pool is sealed by the power of the cross.

◆ See yourself lying in the centre of the pool, but not at this moment on the cross, and allow the blue light to surround you.

◆ Now physically extend your arms and imagine yourself lying on the cross. Feel the golden rays emanating from it and passing through you. Do not let your mind wander even for a moment from the picture of yourself and the pool.

◆ Feel yourself becoming submerged in the pulsating pool of blue light and mentally say to yourself five times: 'This is the sacred pool and I am filled with the power of the golden cross. No harm shall come to me.'

If you re-create the sacred pool of blue light each night before you go to sleep, eventually your dreams should be free of malevolence. However, should no change occur, you should move on to the next exercise.

Externalising the imagination

◆ Each night before you re-create your sacred pool, spend a few moments lying peacefully in a relaxed position, breathing slowly and gently, until your mind is still and serene.

◆ Imagine a tall, strong, friendly figure looking down on you while towering over you in a protective stance. This figure can take any form you like, as long as it is strong and powerful, overwhelmingly friendly towards you and feels as though it belongs to you. You may not wish to create a human form – a powerful animal such as a bear or a lion or something similar will suffice, as long as you feel comfortable with it and know it to be your friend and protector.

◆ Once you have created this protective thought form, begin to re-create your sacred pool of blue light in front of it. When you picture yourself lying on the golden cross in the sacred pool, see yourself being watched over by your friend and protector.

◆ Spend as long as it takes to familiarise yourself with the exercise, then allow yourself to drift gently into the realms of slumber, to dream peaceful dreams without any threat of danger.

I should also say that you must know everything about your silent protector. (It should be silent in order to encourage your visualisation process.) Memorise the features, the shape of the face, the eyes and nose. Know every characteristic, every feeling, and even endeavour to create a personal fragrance for your protector. Animate it and endow it with intelligence. You can do this by talking to it and imagine it responding telepathically.

Over the nights that follow, programme your protector by telling it to guide and protect you while you sleep. Build your relationship slowly, until you feel a deep affinity for your protector.

The only cautionary note I would add is that you should create your silent protector in your mind *only* while you are in your bedroom preparing to sleep. This is a vital part of the programming. In this way your silent protector knows that it is to follow you in sleep only, and in those realms it must remain faithfully by your side.

It is difficult for some people to understand just how effective such an exercise in mind power can actually be. But the menaces encountered during sleep are often created out of the potent substances of the lower astral planes, so it is from these very substances that you must create the weapons to protect yourself.

Most psychic attacks are superficial and will have only a transitory effect on your life. Nonetheless, the effect can be cumulative, so you should never ignore any signs of fatigue or depression.

Keeping Your Family Spiritually Safe

Although strictly speaking a psychic attack on you will not harm your family, it can produce unpleasant feelings around the home.

For this reason you should work on the premise that a psychic attack will also affect your family, and take precautions to safeguard them.

It is important to psychically cleanse the atmosphere in your home occasionally to prevent a build-up of negative energy. The process I am going to suggest is simple yet extremely effective, and is based on the ancient Eastern method of 'perfuming the atmosphere'.

Lavender is the ideal fragrance for this. Not only does it have a calming effect on a stressed and tired mind, but it also has a cleansing effect on the psychic air. Although lavender incense is available in the shops, I find it a little too heavy for cleansing, and prefer to use a lavender room-freshening spray. These are available in most major stores on the high street.

Perfuming the atmosphere

♦ After ensuring that the carpets, floors and walls are free of dust, open all the windows and draw back the curtains, allowing as much natural light and fresh air into the house as possible. Do this even in the winter, if only for a short while.

♦ Play some soothing music, either classical or gentle meditative music.

♦ Spray the lavender in all the rooms, beginning with the corners and concluding with the centre, directing the spray upward to the ceiling.

♦ As you spray, imagine that you are releasing a powerful perfume that will dissolve all negative energy and keep your house free of evil and all psychic germs.

♦ Visualise the lavender particles carrying a powerful cleansing force.

♦ You should take time over the whole process, treating all the rooms that are used most often in the house – the bedrooms, living room and kitchen.

Also, as a cluttered room represents a cluttered mind, it is important to keep the rooms you live in fairly tidy, and for best and most effective results repeat the cleansing process at least once a month.

Although you should always be aware of the possibility of psychic attack, you now have the basic tools to deal with one should it ever happen. Try not to be influenced too much by other people's ideas of psychic attack, and avoid reading about fictional instances. Be your own guide, and most of all trust your own intuition and judgement.

Conclusion: The Next Steps

Life is a noise that breaks the silence, a noise that soon will pass
BUDDHA

Now that you have successfully completed the 10-step psychic development programme you should feel a sense of achievement. Whether you choose to use your newly developed skills as a professional medium or psychic or simply to gain greater control of your life, you can take your next steps with confidence.

Once you have fully explored the programme and you are satisfied with the results, you may apply your skills to every area of your life. In any situation you will find your perception more acute and your judgement more accurate. Regardless of what type of work you do, the 10-step programme will help you derive more enjoyment from the most arduous of tasks, and to cope better in stressful situations. It has worked for thousands of people, and continues to work for me today.

However, once you have reached a satisfactory point in your development, you must not become complacent and start to think that there is no longer any need to maintain your training. In the same way that you train regularly in the gym to maintain your physical strength, so you need to continue to use the programme to maintain the strength of your psychic faculties.

As time goes on, you may find that you will need to modify your training programme a little, perhaps adapt it to suit your new psychic capabilities or integrate more advanced exercises to increase your powers even more. As I have said many times throughout this book, practice makes perfect. Be consistent with your training, though do not make it a labour, as this defeats the whole object of the exercise.

Remember ...

Meditation

Remember to integrate meditation into your daily routine. Development is an endless process, and meditation is the tool with which you should sharpen your faculties, a tool that should not be allowed to become dull and blunt.

Choose the method of meditation that suits you, even if this means creating it yourself rather than following one of the given styles. As long as it works for you, then it is the method you should use.

Follow your intuition

Take every opportunity to exercise your intuition in everyday life. Make a detailed analysis of people and situations, and always endeavour to 'guess' the outcome of events.

To aid the development of your intuition, always exercise your mind as much as possible. When you need to remember something, avoid writing it down, as this only makes the memory lazy and sluggish. If you file things carefully in your memory, it will become efficient and reliable. The more you use it, the more effective it will become. And the stronger the memory, the more powerful the mind.

Using your Psychic Skills

Having completed my programme, decide what you would like to achieve next. Take a notebook and make a detailed plan of how you would like to use your psychic skills. Give yourself some alternatives, set yourself some goals and create a working schedule for the rest of the year.

You may feel that you would like to pass on what you have learned from the programme, and you may find yourself being asked to talk about your achievements or even teach your skills to others. Once the psychic abilities are fully developed, amazing things often do happen, and you may find yourself drawn towards others who will look to you for knowledge and guidance. Although the precept 'When the student is ready the teacher will always appear' often becomes a reality, in many cases the student becomes the teacher.

However, whatever course you choose to pursue, do not rush blindly into a decision. Be patient and wait to see what happens and which way you are guided.

Working as a psychic

More people than you might imagine think that being psychic is an alternative to actually working for a living. For me personally, it is nice to be doing a job that I actually enjoy, but it is certainly not an easy way to make a living, as it is both mentally and physically draining.

Although I could make an extremely comfortable living just doing private consultations, I choose not to do so. I know some clairvoyants who do nothing but readings from 10 a.m. until 7 p.m., day in and day out, six days a week, client after client, almost on a conveyer belt. Personally, I not only think this is very unhealthy for the clairvoyant, I also can't believe that reading after reading can be reliable. One reading would begin to merge with the next, eventually causing the brain to become numb. Should giving readings all day be your plan, I would seriously suggest that you reconsider.

This issue aside, you need the clientele to make a professional psychic career viable, and until your psychic skills have been developed to a fairly high standard you will have to wait for that never-ending queue of clients. However, you will know when you have attained that standard by the number of times your telephone rings in any one day.

Again, if you are drawn to working in this area, be patient and see whether opportunities arise for you.

Healing skills

Should healing be your primary interest, then application is necessary in order for your skills to develop. Remember, regardless of what type of healing you are giving, it is a process that requires compassion, sincerity and dedication.

When administering healing, always be aware of personal hygiene and take care to eliminate strong bodily odours that your patients may find offensive. Whether healing or working as a psychic in a one-to-one situation, a pleasant fragrance will not only please the senses of the person with whom you are working, but will also be reassuring if they are nervous or finding it difficult to relax.

The skills you have mastered on the 10-step programme will not only change your own life, they will also affect those with whom you come into contact. The 10-step programme is about the development of your spiritual consciousness as well as your psychic faculties, and the spiritual mind is warm, compassionate and alive with high feeling. Once you have attained a satisfactory degree of spiritual awareness, you will find yourself drawing, like a magnet, those with similar aspirations, placing you in the all-important position of teacher, able to help others in their thirst for knowledge.

I for one wish you well in your future work, and sincerely hope it brings you the happiness, contentment and peace of mind that mine has brought me.

Afterword: Spiritual Awakening

Of all the words in the vocabulary of those endeavouring to develop their psychic skills, 'spiritual' is undoubtedly the most misused and misunderstood. In fact, I wish I had a pound for every time I have heard someone proudly proclaim 'I am very spiritual!' when they actually mean 'very psychic', or ask 'I am quite spiritual, do you think I should develop it further?' Rightly or wrongly, I usually humour them. But what does the word 'spiritual' really mean, and how does spiritual awakening relate to developing your psychic skills?

To say that you have awoken spiritually suggests that you have developed a deeper awareness of God. This can come through many years of seeking enlightenment, either through prayer, meditation and devotion, or perhaps more spontaneously as the result of a traumatic experience.

During the course of my work I have met many people who are only too eager to tell me what they have achieved spiritually, what they can do and whom they have healed. I have heard such accounts so many times over the past 25 years that now the word 'spiritual' sticks in my throat and I feel embarrassed at the mere mention of it. I have become very cynical about such statements, and wonder sometimes about people's own perception of themselves.

Maurice Maeterlinck obviously had his own feelings about such people when he wrote in his little book *Treasure of the Humble*, 'Only when the lips are still shall the soul arise to set forth on its labours.' Maeterlinck's observations had obviously led him to believe that spirituality must be kept secret and allowed to work in the quiet recesses of the soul. In fact, later on in the book, he speaks clearly and profoundly about the dawning of spirituality and likens it to discovering gems:

> *It is as though you had dived to the most unfathomable depths, and yet when you return to the surface, the drop of water that glistens at your fingertips no longer resembles the sea from which it came. You may think that you have discovered a beautiful grotto, filled with a magnificent treasure, only to find that when you return to the light of day, the gems you have brought back with you are false – mere pieces of glass! And yet, how that treasure shines on unceasingly in the darkness.*

I must say that Maeterlinck's observations and insights have certainly helped me in my own spiritual search.

If I am truthful with myself, I do not feel any different now than I did before I started my work. But then, according to higher teachings, if I were to feel different, I would not have achieved anything. I do know, however, that I have a much deeper awareness of both other people and life in general. Whether or not that can be defined as 'spiritual' is another matter. All I can say is that exploring different religions, in particular the Eastern traditions, has helped me immensely to understand why I do what I do, and why exactly I have had the experiences I have.

Beginning with a Single Step

When I think of spiritual development, certain ancient precepts spring to mind. One of them is: 'The thousand-mile journey begins with a single step'. You will never transform spiritually until you make a conscious decision to actually begin the process. Another is: 'He who rides the tiger's back dare not dismount'. How true this is, for when the process begins, it can neither be abandoned nor suspended, but must reach a natural conclusion.

By now you may be wondering what, if anything, all this has got to do with the process of psychic development. But as I said at the very beginning, once you have embarked upon the process of psychic development, a deeper spiritual understanding must also evolve. Without this understanding, as the psychic faculties begin to develop, complications are bound to arise.

As Maeterlinck said, 'The wise man is not he who sees, but he who, seeing furthest, has the greatest love and understanding for all mankind. He who sees without loving and understanding is only straining his eyes in the darkness.'

Spiritual understanding gives you a different perspective and allows your emotions to become actively involved in everything that you do. For example, I have been a vegetarian since I was 14 years old. At that time vegetarianism was unheard of in a working-class family in Liverpool, where the traditional 'Scouse' meal of meat was an integral part of the weekly diet. Although my mother made every effort to make me eat some meat, I always declined, claiming that it made me sick – which, of course, it did. Tall Pine once said to me, 'You cannot caress an animal with one hand and pick its bones with the other. He who has the courage to kill the animal has the spiritual right to consume its flesh.' This made sense to me even at the age of 14. I could not kill an animal, so why should I eat the flesh of one?

It all began because I saw three creatures killed in quick succession. First of all I witnessed a young boy on the beach purposely jump on a crab as it tried to make its way back into the sea. Then I saw a blackbird killed by a speeding car in Sefton Park. Finally I witnessed two boys corner a frightened mouse, and I could only watch helplessly as they killed it with a brick. These horrific sights have remained with me and have been catalysts in my life and the whole process of my developing sensitivity. They were undoubtedly signposts along my way.

To me, vegetarianism means much more than abstaining from the consumption of meat – it is a deep understanding that it is spiritually wrong to eat the flesh of a living creature. I get annoyed when I hear the sceptic saying, 'That's what cows and sheep are for!' or 'Jesus ate meat!' That does not necessarily make it right. If we are never to move away from the archaic ways of biblical figures then we will never evolve spiritually. Besides, we don't know for sure that Jesus did eat meat, but we do know that, according to Judaic traditions, it was normal to indulge in the barbaric slaughter of a sacrificial lamb. I do not think there is anything godly, spiritual or religious in that practice.

I don't mean this to be 'super-spiritual', and I'm not implying that everyone should follow the same course of action as part of my programme. However, vegetarianism is advocated by yogic masters, the idea being that it raises the vibrations of the soul.

The Threefold Path of the Lotus

Eastern traditions compare the soul's evolutionary process to the growth of the lotus flower, which goes through three different stages:

1. The roots of the lotus are deeply embedded in the mud at the bottom of a pool, while the flower stem reaches up through the mud – a symbolic representation of the earth upon which we live. As we grow spiritually, we begin to understand that the planet is a living organism – she lives, she breathes, she feels.

2. The stem of the lotus flower moves from the mud into the water – a symbolic representation of our emotions. As we develop spiritually, so we become more emotionally sensitive. We begin to cultivate compassion, love and kindness towards others.

3. Finally, the flower opens up into the air – a symbolic representation of our mentality. We begin to understand

the true nature of the world and realise that by training our minds we can achieve our full potential.

Learning from Experience

Some years ago now, at a time when I could not function without some form of narcotic to sustain me, at probably the lowest point of my life, I had the saddest and yet most significant experience in the development of my spiritual understanding.

It was New Year's Eve, 1970, and I found myself wandering aimlessly through the streets of Wavertree, the district where I was born and grew up. It was about 11.30 p.m., but I was only vaguely aware of the cacophony of music spilling into the streets and the general merriment of revellers dancing.

I found myself standing at the front door of the home of one of my oldest friends, and could see that inside there was a party in full swing. I knocked loudly on the door and within moments a young woman opened it. 'I'm a friend of Peter's,' I said, smiling and expecting to be asked in. I saw Peter's head peep round the living-room door, but then I heard him say, 'We'll have no luck all year if he comes in.' My heart just sank and I turned and walked away. I felt quite numb inside and could not control the tears as they trickled down my icy cheeks.

Although this was a small incident, it was a major event in my spiritual development. It brought me great sadness, but it made me realise who I actually was, and at that moment I wanted so much to change. I have never forgotten that experience. My friend, of course, has no recollection of it whatsoever. He wouldn't, would he?

So often it is the small, seemingly insignificant incidents in life which aid us in our development and help us realise that we reap what we sow. In fact, if we accept the spiritual law of karma, of cause and effect, then we can see that we are constantly working through our imperfections, putting right our mistakes. And so the spiritual 'path of attainment' is available to everyone, and everyone must ultimately walk it.

Spirit Guides and Guardian Angels

It is a pleasant thought that we are not alone on the path, however, but are looked after by exalted beings who guide us safely through the turbulent rapids of life. There are most definitely angelic forces at work, and whether you call them 'spirit guides' or 'guardian angels', there is absolutely no doubt in my mind that they are supervising the evolution of our souls.

I am often asked why these spirit guides nearly always seem to be Native American, monks or nuns. The simple answer to that question is that they are not. Native Americans were in fact very close to the earth and often interested in the spiritual well-being of mankind, and many monks and nuns do want to continue their spiritual work after death, but the truth is that the outward persona of our guides is one that we ourselves choose. Very often these spiritual beings have never experienced an earthly existence and only take on these human forms in order to make us feel comfortable as they further our understanding.

For many years my work as a medium was predominantly controlled by a group of discarnate souls known to me as 'the Elders'. As far as I knew they were spirit guides, some of whom had never experienced a physical life. More than this I did not know. It wasn't until the early eighties that I discovered, just by chance, that the Elders were in fact facets of a single personality – Tall Pine, the gentle soul who had helped me throughout my life. Although I had grown up thinking that Tall Pine was a North American tribesman, I was surprised to learn that this was in fact simply the persona he presented to me, and that his true identity was yet to be revealed. However, today I still look upon TP as a Native American, a friend who is there whenever I need him.

A more profound concept of spirit guides is that they are facets of our own being, and that we create them subconsciously out of a deep inherent need. It was once said that if God did not exist we would have to invent Him. The idea of wandering aimlessly through life, completely alone in our spiritual endeavours and aspirations, is quite depressing, I think, and so the idea of having spirit guides, wherever they come from, makes a lot of sense.

Although we have many such beings guiding us, most working mediums tend to relate to one or maybe two of their guides. Personally, as I have explained, I have the deepest affinity with Tall Pine. To me he is very real and as solid and substantial as anyone else in this world. I do not, however, make the mistake of worshipping him as though he were a deity. A spirit guide, of any sort, is merely a representative of God, an ambassador whose only desire is to serve.

Another misconception about spirit guides is that they always guide you down the smoothest road, with the intention of making life easy for you. This is not so. They are as much on the path of attainment as we are. As we grow spiritually, so do they. I know from my own life that in order for us to gain more experience our guides very often take us down the rockiest road. This is how our consciousness expands and we grow spiritually.

I have no doubt that there are also other souls watching over all of us, but that these choose to do their work anonymously, from the shadows, as it were. These are not necessarily highly evolved beings, just simple souls with aspirations towards helping the human race on the long path of spiritual attainment.

Spirit Messages

As you become more spiritually aware, your mind somehow becomes more attuned to souls in the spirit world who may want to communicate spiritual truths to you. You may occasionally be overwhelmed by the urge to write, even though you may never have written before. Thoughts may pour into your mind seemingly from nowhere, and when they are put down on paper they may appear to be a spirit message.

Some years ago now, on a very cold November afternoon, I was sitting sleepily in front of the coal fire in the living room of my mother's house, listening to the wind howling fiercely down the chimney. As I gazed through the window I could see amber clouds in a clear blue sky, and I felt very relaxed. Suddenly I found myself sitting bolt upright in the chair with my heart pounding inside my chest. I felt compelled to get a pen and paper and write down all the strange words passing through my mind. I wrote the following poem without even thinking about what I was writing.

Death is not the end, but the beginning

A dead man's poem

> Oh pallid death of shadow and mystery! What secret dost thou
> conceal behind thy pale mask? Would that I could have betrayed
> all that thou did ask of my aged form, that I my span might
> have lived once more.
>
> Alas! In betraying thee the better I could have betrayed myself.
> In that, all that I was in life I was because of thee. Oh,
> messenger of dread and darkness, whose eager face never was I
> to see, nor dull voice ever to hear above the hush of silence that
> muffled thy footsteps as they drew near to my fading heart, as I
> upon my bed thy touch did silently await.

And so, I looked upon that alone which thou would have me gaze on. The shadow of the cause, which I in life had sought to embrace, and the face of each and every man, for whom I through ambition had no regard, tauntingly passed before my tired mind.

And so in this world of twilight do I reside with contemplation and deep thought, to find that with my God shall I abide till all his lessons have been taught. At least then shall I be free ...

I have since learned that a wealthy Victorian writer transmitted this poem to me psychically. He had wrongly assumed that death was the end, and in life had no regard for anyone but himself. The strongest memories he had of his death were of lying on his sickbed waiting for the 'angel of death' to call, his whole life flashing painfully through his mind. Once he had made the transition from this world to the next, he realised that his worldly wealth was worthless in the world of spirit, and before he could move on through the worlds of the cosmos he had to make amends to those for whom he had had little regard.

Although he communicated with me numerous times between 1983 and 1985, he never told me his name. It occurred to me, however, that he and I were one and the same, and that I had been him at a different time, perhaps in a different place, and that we had shared the same thoughts and experienced the same feelings. I really do have the overwhelming feeling that I am the re-embodiment of that man, that I have returned to fulfil some part of my life that was then lacking.

Reincarnation

We are born more than once, and each birth brings us nearer to
God. And even as we walk this life the hands of our ancestors
are clasped by the hands of our brothers and our sons yet
unborn.

MAURICE MAETERLINCK

How can we possibly learn enough in one lifetime? Three score years
and ten is far too short a time to reach our full spiritual potential, and
most certainly not enough time in which to achieve God-like
perfection.

Although reincarnation is not included in modern Christian
teachings, it formed an integral part of early Christian doctrine, and
it is still one of the fundamental principles of Eastern religions. But
if reincarnation is a fact, which part of us is actually reborn, and is
reincarnation compulsory?

There are many theories about reincarnation, but most agree that
it is not compulsory but rather a choice made because of the soul's
need for experience. The individual may choose their time and place
of birth, circumstances and even the family into which they are
born. This is probably why we sometimes witness an extremely well-
adjusted, kind and honest individual in a family of rogues and
villains, or a dishonest thug born to good and honest parents. The
dishonest will influence the honest, and the honest will affect the
dishonest, and each will help the other in the struggle to truly be
themselves.

The doctrine of reincarnation is strongly supported by the theory
of karma, the law of cause and effect, as one cannot operate without
the other. As we learn this, we can begin to take greater responsibility for our actions.

In fact, I have always had it instilled in me by the Elders that the motive is more important than the action, and if the motive is not right, the action will not produce the correct effect.

Looking Forward

In his book *The 14 Lessons in Yogi Philosophy and Oriental Occultism*, the mystic Yogi Ramacharaka wrote: 'As man unfolds in spiritual consciousness, he begins to have an abiding sense of the reality of the existence of the Supreme Power. And growing along with this he finds that sense of human brotherhood, of human relationship, gradually coming into consciousness.'

This was written in 1903, at a time when psychic matters were viewed with some suspicion in the West and spirituality was left primarily to the Church and its representatives.

Today, however, as we move into the Age of Aquarius, a whole new concept of spirituality is beginning to unfold. The human race as a whole is now entering a new spiritual epoch. Children born within this age will possess psychic and spiritual skills the like of which will never have been witnessed before. Even over the last ten years or so interest in esoteric and metaphysical traditions has increased, and we are witnessing children as young as three years old with unusual creative and intellectual abilities. There is an invisible power propelling the human race forward, and each and every soul is struggling towards the light.

I hope that this book has helped you in some way on your own journey. Each person achieves something different in the process of psychic development, and yet the results can touch every area of your life. The rewards can be endless, though the process is not always easy. Tall Pine once said to me, 'Tread and search carefully. Leave no stone unturned, for although there are many treasures yet to be discovered, there are innumerable rocky defiles through which you must pass – all of which are within your own nature.'

The treasures to which Tall Pine refers are, of course, the treasures of the spirit, and, as Maurice Maeterlinck said, that particular treasure 'shines on unceasingly in the darkness'. I hope that this programme will help you find many such treasures and to live a fuller and richer life. I wish you well in your journey, and hope that you will contact me to let me know what you have achieved.

Colour Glossary

The healing properties of colour were known to the ancients of Egypt, who used coloured gauze to filter and direct the sun's rays to the afflicted person. This therapy was regarded as specialised and highly scientific, and was extremely effective in the treatment of diseases of both the body and the mind.

Colour can in fact be used in the treatment of disease in various ways. The patient may be bathed in the appropriate coloured light for short periods of time, or water may poured into different-coloured tumblers, left standing for a short while, and then consumed. This process encourages the revitalisation of prana, allowing the water to be more susceptible to the sun's rays.

Another simple and yet extremely effective way in which colour may be used is for the patient to sleep in the appropriate coloured sheet. For example, red to give warmth and stimulate the blood, blue to lower the temperature and soothe inflammation. A little experimentation is always recommended.

Although the whole process of healing with colour may be achieved by mentally transmitting their various shades and degrees, treatment is far more effective with the use of a lamp with different coloured bulbs. Although it is possible to buy a lamp specifically designed for colour treatment, ordinary electric lamps with 200 watt bulbs will suffice. Likewise, if it is not possible to use infrared and ultraviolet lamps, simultaneous use of red and blue bulbs is nearly always just as effective.

In deciding what colours to use, you should find the list below helpful.

Colours and the Conditions They Affect

Abscesses – Indigo

Adrenals – Blue

Anaemia – Red

Blood poisoning – Red

Blood pressure (high) – Blue or Purple

Blood pressure (low) – Magenta

Blood purification – Indigo

Boils – Indigo

Bone disease – Violet

Bronchitis – Blue and Green

Cancer – Blue

Circulation (poor) – Red

Colds – Red

Congestion – Violet

Constipation – Yellow

Exhaustion – bright Red, with Yellow and Orange

Eyesight (poor) – Green

Fevers – Blue or Indigo

Hair (thinning) – Violet

Hardening of the arteries – Ultraviolet

Hay fever – Green

Headaches – Blue

Heart (weak) – Red

Heart diseases – Indigo and/or Violet

Influenza – Red and Blue

Insanity – Yellow and Blue

Jaundice – Red and Green

Kidney disease – Yellow, Blue and Violet

Liver diseases – Green

Lungs – Orange

Malaria – Green

Muscles (weak) – Indigo

Nerves (revitalising) – Yellow and Green

Nerves (soothing) – Violet, Lavender and Gold

Nerves (stimulation) – Red and Green

Organic disease – Blue

Over-stimulation of the mind – Green

Pneumonia – Blue, Red and Violet

Poisons in the body – Green and Blue

Psychic problems – Indigo, Blue and Violet

Rheumatism – Indigo

Scalp conditions – Blue or Violet

Sciatica – Blue

Skin problems – Blue and Indigo

Stomach conditions – Indigo and Violet

Tuberculosis – Yellow and Blue

Underweight – Green

Veins (varicose) – Blue and Indigo

Character traits, qualities and emotions and the colours they produce in the aura

Although actually 'seeing' the aura does allow you to gain access to a whole new and exciting world of knowledge and information, about things and other people, interpretation of the colours, both individually and collectively, is paramount. The way in which one person perceives red, for example, is not necessarily the way you perceive it. Once colour has been registered by the retina of your eyes, you must then allow your intuition to translate and interpret. Although you may see red in a person's aura, your intuition may interpret this as warmth and strength, and not as anger or volatility. You may see red combined with a gentle shade of green. It is important not to make too detailed an analysis of this combination, but to allow your intuition to spontaneously interpret the meaning transmitted. Your eyes will receive only the colour transmitted, but your intuitive consciousness will translate it. It is important not to be discouraged once you have made an assessment of someone's aura, and always stand by your final conclusions.

Adoration – Green

Affection – Rich dark Blue

Ambition – Deep Orange

Anger – Varying degrees and shades of Red

Animal instincts – A dull shade of Red with Grey or Brown

Animal passions – Dark Red and Crimson

Attainment (spiritual or intellectual) – Gold with Blue

Avarice – Reddish Brown and dark Green

Awakened spirituality – Pure White

Brutality – Flashes of bright Red with dark Brown

Business-minded – Orange with golden Brown

Charitable – Light translucent Green

Clairvoyant skill – Orchid or Aquamarine

Compassion – Pale Green and Pink

Confidence – Bright blue or clear Orange

Courage (lacking) – Varying shades of Grey

Courage – Bright Orange

Critical – Bright Yellow

Cruel – Cloudy Red

Cunning – Brick Red with mustard Yellow

Deceitful – Dirty Green to lemon Green

Defiant – Jade Green with Scarlet

Depression – Varying degrees of Grey with Brown

Desire (lustful) – Crimson

Desire for sympathy – Green with Red

Devotion – Mauve or Blue

Diplomacy – Varying shades of jade Green

Discord (mental) – Black and dark Grey

Domineering – Dark Red

Egotistical – Scarlet

Energy (physical) – Bright clear Red

Envy – Deep Red, dark Green; Red with flashes of Green

Evil – Black

Extrovert – Varying degrees of Orange

Faith (religious) – Royal Blue

Falsehood (liar) – Green with lemon flashes over head

Fear – Varying shades and degrees of Grey with Black

Friendliness – Golden Yellow

Generous nature – Rose Pink

Gloomy – Black or deep Grey

Greed – Cloudy Red; reddish Brown

Happiness – Golden Yellow and Pink

Hatred – Red flashes on Black; Black clouds and dark Red

Healing power – Bright emerald Green or deep Blue

High spirits – Pale Yellow

Home-loving – Soft Green or Rose

Ignorance – Grey or Black

Impractical – Dull Yellow

Independent – Bright Green

Indignation (righteous) – Scarlet flashes

Ingenuity – Emerald Green or bright Yellow

Inspiration – Blue or Aquamarine

Intellect – Yellow

Intuition – Pure Yellow or bright Blue with Yellow flashes

Irritation – Light Scarlet

Jealous anger – Blood Red

Jealousy – Brownish Green, Scarlet flecks on Brown, dark Green with reddish brown

Joyousness – Rose Pink

Lethargy – Grey or cloudy Blue

Logical reasoning – Clear golden Yellow

Love – Crimson Pink or bright Pink

Love (spiritual) – Pure Yellow; Gold or bright Pink with Blue

Low desires – Crimson

Lust – Deep Scarlet

Malice – Smoky Grey or Black

Melancholy – Dark, cloudy Grey

Mental activity – Apple Green

Murderous passion – Blood Red

Narrow-mindedness – Cloudy Grey

Negative thinking – Dirty Grey

Over-indulgence – Dark, cloudy Orange

Peaceful – Soft, clear Green

Perfection – White

Pessimism – Cloudy Black or slate Grey

Politeness – Jade Green with Coral

Power (spiritual) – Violet

Power (worldly) – Bright Orange

Pride (egotistical) – Scarlet with shades of cloudy Blue

Pride (intellectual) – Bright Orange, sometimes Gold

Psychic powers (evil) – Infrared

Rage – Murky Red or dirty Green

Religious feeling – Blue or Violet

Renunciation of self – Pale Blue

Revenge – Blood Red, cloudy Black

Secretiveness – Cloud Grey or Black

Self-centredness – Light Red with cloudy Grey

Self-control – Golden or bright Orange

Selfishness – Cloudy Brown with dirty Green and reddish Brown

Sensual desire – Dark and cloudy Red

Serenity – Rich Blue or Aquamarine

Sex desire – Crimson

Suspicion – Dirty Yellow

Sympathy – Bright Pink, translucent Green

Temper – Dark Red with Scarlet flashes

Timidity – Yellow and reddish Brown

Universal brotherhood – Rose Pink, sometimes bright Aquamarine

Universal love – Rose Pink with Gold

Unselfish love – Pale Rose with pale Green

Vitality – Clear, translucent Red

Wisdom – Gold and dark Blue

Glossary of Useful Sanskrit Words

AJNA – Brow chakra

ANAHATA – Heart chakra

ASANA – Bodily posture in yoga

ASHRAM – Centre for religious study

ATMAN – The real immortal self, the soul

BHAGAVAD GITA – Considered to be the 'Gospel' of Hinduism

BIJA – Energy, seed, root power

BINDU – Particle, dot, spot; focal point for concentration

BUDDHA – 'Awakened one'

CHAKRA – Wheel or circle; psychic centre

CHI – Air, vapour, breath, ether, energy

DEVA – Shining one

DHYANA – Meditation, absorption

DIVYA SIDDHIS – Supernatural powers

EKADASHI – The eleventh day following a full or new moon, a day of prayer

GANESHA – Son of Shiva, god of wisdom

GOMATI – Full of light

GURU – Teacher or spiritual master

HATHA YOGA – Physical postures to attain spiritual and physical well-being, hatha meaning male and female, yoga meaning union

IDA – One of the primary channels of subtle energy, the female aspect

INDRA – God of the firmament, the personified atmosphere; the supreme deity, lord of weather

JIVA – A mortal being

KALACHAKRA – 'Wheel of time'

KAMA – Sensual desire, longing, sexual pleasure

KAMALOKA – Triloka; three worlds, three spheres

KAMA-SUTRA – 'Manual of the erotic art'

KARMA – 'Deed'; the sum of all consequences of an individual's actions in this or previous incarnations

KASINA – 'Total field' objects of meditation

KUNDALINI – 'Snake' or 'Serpent Power'; spiritual force coiled at the base of the spine

LAMA – In Buddhism a religious master or guru

LAYA – Dissolution, disappearance of self; the merging of the individual soul with the absolute; union with God

LOKA – 'World'

LOTUS – Plant of the waterlily family, a symbolic representation of various levels of consciousness

MAHARISHI – 'Great seer'

MAHATMA – 'Great soul'

MAHAVIRA – 'Great hero"

MAHAYANA – 'Great vehicle'

MAITRI – 'Kindness', 'benevolence'

MAITRI-KARUNA – 'Kindness and compassion'

MANAS – 'Mind'; capacity for thought

MANDALA – 'Circle' symbolising cosmic forces

MANIPURA – Third chakra

MANTRA (also Mantram) – Power-laden syllable or series of syllables to be chanted

MAYA – 'Illusion' or 'deception'

MUDRA – 'Seal', 'sign'; symbolic hand postures

MULADHARA – First chakra

NADI – 'Nerve', 'vessel' or 'vein'; channels through which pranic energy flows

NIRVANA – 'Extinction'; a state of illumination; the highest state of consciousness, the goal of meditation

OM or AUM – The symbol of form as well as sound; considered to be the manifestation of spiritual power

OM MANI PADME HUM – 'Om, the Jewel in the Lotus'; meaningful and very powerful mantra

PINGALA – One of the three important channels that convey prana throughout the body; the male aspect

PRANA – 'Breath', 'breath of life'; the subtle agent through which the life of the body is sustained

PRANAYAMA – 'The control of prana'; the yogic system of breath control

RAJA YOGA – 'The Royal Yoga'

SAHASRARA – Seventh chakra

SAMADHI – 'Establish', 'make firm'; state of consciousness that lies beyond waking and dreaming, where all mental activity ceases

SAMSARA – 'Journeying'; cycle of birth, death and rebirth

SAMUDRA – 'Ocean'; streams of higher consciousness

SAMYAMA – 'Restraint', 'self-control'

SANSKRIT – Sacred language of Hinduism

SHAKTI – 'Force', 'power', 'energy'

SHAMA – Control of the mind through a process of undivided concentration; object of meditation

SHAMATHA – 'Dwelling in tranquillity'

SHANTA – 'Inner peace'

SHANTI – 'Peace'

SHARIRA – 'Body', 'husk'

SHRAVANA – 'Hearing', 'learning'

SIDDHI – 'Perfect abilities'; psychic or supernatural abilities

SUSHUMNA – Subtle energy channel, extending from the base of the spine to the brain

SVADISTHANA – Second chakra

TANTRA – 'Weft', 'context', 'continuum'

TANTRA YOGA – Synonymous with kundalini yoga

TATTVA – 'Truth', 'true being', 'fundamental principle'

TRATAKA – To focus the attention on a specific spot

UPANISHADS – Upa: 'near'; ni: 'down'; sad: 'sit'; to sit down near to; at the feet of a guru; sacred writings derived from the Vedas

VAYU – 'Air', 'wind'

VEDAS – 'Knowledge', 'sacred teaching'

VISHUDDA – Fifth chakra

YANTRA – Geometric shape or design; 'support', 'instrument'; focal point for meditation

YOGA – 'Yoke'; process of unifying the male and female energies with the divine

YOGA-SHAKTI – Powers gained through the physical disciplines of yoga

Further Reading

Jack Angelo and Jan Angelo, *Your Healing Power*, Piatkus Books, 2001

Edwin Babbitt, *Principles of Light and Colour*, R. A. Kessinger Publishing Co, 1940

Douglas Baker, *The Human Aura*, Baker Publications, 1986

——*Superconsciousness through Meditation*, Aquarian, 1978

L. J. Bendit and P. D. Payne, *The Etheric Body of Man*, Quest Books, 1996

Annie Besant, *Thought Power*, R. A. Kessinger Publishing Co, 1997

——and C. W. Leadbeater, *Thought Forms*, Quest Books, 1995

James Hewitt, *The Complete Yoga Book*, Rider, 1991

Kay Hoffman, *The Trance Workshop Book*, Sterling Publishing, 2000

Dr Kilner, *The Aura* (also known as *The Human Atmosphere*), R. A. Kessinger Publishing Co, 1996

C. W. Leadbeater, *The Chakras*, Theosophical Publishing House, 1927

Tre McCamley, *Palm Decoder*, Aurum Press, 1999

Maurice Maeterlinck, *Treasure of the Humble*, Ams Press, 1988

——*Wisdom and Destiny*, University Press of the Pacific, 2001

R. Morris, *Achilles in the Quantum Universe*, Souvenir Press, 1998

A. E. Powell, *The Etheric Double*, Theosophical Publishing House, 1969

Yogi Ramacharaka, *Gnani Yoga*, The C. W. Daniel Company Ltd, 1963

——*Hatha Yoga*, The C. W. Daniel Company Ltd, 1963

——*Life beyond Death*, R. A. Kessinger Publishing Co, 1912

——*Psychic Healing*, R. A. Kessinger Publishing Co, 1906

——*Series of Lessons in Raja Yoga*, R. A. Kessinger Publishing Co, 1906

——The Science of Breath, R. A. Kessinger Publishing Co, 1904
Billy Roberts, Working Memory, Alison & Busby, 2000
Simon Tomlin, The Unexplained – Psychic Powers, Parragon, 2000
Ruth White, Working with Your Chakras, Piaktus Books, 1993

Index

Index